CASE STUDY RESEARCH IN EDUCATIONAL SETTINGS

DOING QUALITATIVE RESEARCH IN EDUCATIONAL SETTINGS

Series Editor: Pat Sikes

The aim of this series is to provide a range of high quality introductory research methods texts. Each volume focuses, critically, on one particular methodology enabling a detailed yet accessible discussion. All of the contributing authors are established researchers with substantial, practical experience. While every book has its own unique style, each discusses the historical background of the approach, epistemological issues and appropriate uses. They then go on to describe the operationalisation of the approach in educational settings drawing upon specific and vivid examples from the authors' own work. The intention is that readers should come away with a level of understanding that enables them to feel sufficiently confident to undertake their own research as well as to critically evaluate other accounts of research using the approach.

Published titles

Michael Bassey: *Case Study Research in Educational Settings*
Morwenna Griffiths: *Educational Research for Social Justice*

CASE STUDY RESEARCH IN EDUCATIONAL SETTINGS

Michael Bassey

Open University Press
Buckingham · Philadelphia

Open University Press
Celtic Court
22 Ballmoor
Buckingham
MK18 1XW

email: enquiries@openup.co.uk
world wide web: http://www.openup.co.uk

and
325 Chestnut Street
Philadelphia, PA 19106, USA

First Published 1999

A catalogue record of this book is available from the British Library

ISBN   0 335 19984 4 (pb)   0 335 19985 2 (hb)

Library of Congress Cataloging-in-Publication Data
Bassey, Michael
    Case study research in educational settings / Michael Bassey.
        p.   cm. – (Doing qualitative research in educational settings)
    Includes bibliographical references (p.   ) and indexes.
    ISBN 0-335-19984-4 (pbk.). – ISBN 0-335-19985-2 (hard)
    1. Education–Research–Great Britain–Methodology.   2. Case
method.   I. Title.   II. Series.
LB1028.25.G7B37   1999
370'.72–dc21   98-30734
                                                                              CIP

Typeset by Type Study, Scarborough
Printed in Great Britain by Biddles Ltd, Guildford and King's Lynn

Contents

Series editor's preface   viii
Preface   xiii

Part I Reconstruction of educational case study   1

1 Why educational case study should be reconstructed   3
   My experience as an examiner of master's dissertations and
      doctoral theses   5
   My experience of research in the public domain   7
   My writing and thinking about research   11
   A reconstruction of case study   12

**2 An example of a theory-seeking case study leading to fuzzy
   propositions**   14
   Theory in initial teacher education: some BEd students'
      perspectives on its utility in 1996   14

3 What is case study?   22
   Towards a science of the singular   22
   Descriptions of case study given by different writers   23
   Types of case study described by various writers   27
   How the problem of generalization is approached by
      different writers   30
   Academic criticisms of case study   34
   Endpiece   35

**4 Locating educational case study on the map of research in
   education**   37
   What is 'education'?   37
   What is research?   38
   What is educational research?   38
   What is discipline research in educational settings?   39

What is empirical research, and what are its categories? 40
How do different beliefs in the nature of reality affect
    educational case study? 42
What are scientific, statistical and fuzzy generalizations? 44
What is a study of a singularity? 47

5 **How some case study research can be disseminated through
    fuzzy generalization and professional discourse** 48
'Do *y* instead of *x* and your pupils will learn more' 48
Research feeds discourse, which aids practice and policy 49
Fuzzy generalizations as sound bites from research 51
Examples of fuzzy generalizations 53
Putting research reports on the Internet 54
Endpiece 55

6 **Educational case study as a prime strategy for developing
    educational theory which illuminates educational policy and
    enhances educational practice** 57
A conceptual reconstruction of educational case study 57
Rationale for the elements of the reconstruction 59
The categorization of case study in this reconstruction 62

7 **Methods of enquiry and the conduct of case study research** 65
Introduction 65
Stages in conducting case study research 65
The ethics of research 73
Trustworthiness in case study research 74
Respect for persons in case study research 77
Archive, case record and case report 79
Data collection methods 81
Data analysis 83
Writing case reports 84
Audit certificate 90

Part II Examples of case studies 93

Preamble 93

8 **The Nottinghamshire Staff Development Project 1985–1987:
    a story-telling case study about an evaluation** 95
Abstract 95
Introduction 95
Section 1 97
Section 2 110

9 Classroom organization in primary schools: a story-telling
  case study about three theory-seeking case studies and a
  theory-testing survey   116
  Abstract   116
  Introduction   116
  A day in Mrs M's classroom: a theory-seeking case study   117
  A day in Mrs W's classroom: a theory-seeking case study   126
  A day in Mr A's classroom: a theory-seeking case study   140
  A theory of classroom organizational strategies   151
  Endpiece   156

10 What it is like to be a student on final teaching practice: a
   picture-drawing case study of fiction firmly based on fact   158
   Abstract   158
   Preamble   158
   Introduction   159
   How the findings were reported   160
   Internal evidence of trustworthiness   162
   External evidence of trustworthiness   172
   Endpiece   173

References   174
Index   177

Series editor's preface

I had never realized just how fascinating research was in its own right. I was expecting the research methods course to be boring, difficult and all about statistics but I couldn't have been more wrong. There is so much to consider, so many aspects, so many ways of finding out what's going on, and not just one way of representing it too. I have been really surprised.

(Student taking an MA in Educational Studies)

I never knew that there was so much to research. I thought that you just chose a method, applied it, did your statistical sums and came up with your findings. The reality is more complicated but so much more interesting and meaningful.

(Student taking an MA in Educational Studies)

The best thing for me was being told that qualitative research is 'proper' research – providing it's done properly of course. What goes on in schools is so complex and involves so many different perspectives that I think you often need a qualitative approach to begin to get some idea of what's going on.

(Student taking an MA in Sociology)

I really appreciate hearing about other researchers' experiences of doing research. It was quite a revelation when I first became aware that things don't always go as smoothly as some written accounts seem to suggest. It's really reassuring to hear honest reports: they alert you to pitfalls and problems and things that you might not have thought about.

(Doctoral student)

Comments such as these will be familiar to anyone who has ever taught or taken a course which aims to introduce the range of research approaches available to social scientists in general and those working in educational settings in particular.

The central message that they convey seems to be that the influence of the positivist scientist paradigm is both strong and pervasive, shaping expectations of what constitutes 'proper', 'valid' and 'worthwhile' research. What Barry Troyna wrote in 1994, continues to be the case; namely that:

> There is a view which is already entrenched and circulating widely in the populist circles . . . that qualitative research is subjective, value-laden and, therefore, unscientific and invalid, in contrast to quantitative research, which meets the criteria of being objective, value-free, scientific and therefore valid.
>
> (1994: 9)

Within academic and research circles though, where the development of post-modernist and post-structuralist ideas have affected both thinking and research practice, it can be easy to forget what the popular perspective is. This is because, in these communities, qualitative researchers from the range of theoretical standpoints, utilize a variety of methods, approaches, strategies and techniques in the full confidence that their work is rigorous, legitimate and totally justifiable as research. And the process of peer review serves to confirm that confidence.

Recently, however, for those concerned with and involved in research in educational settings, and especially for those engaged in educational research, it seems that the positivist model, using experimental, scientific, quantitative methods, is definitely in the ascendancy once again. Those of us working in England and Wales, go into the new millennium with the government endorsed exhortation to produce evidence-based research which,

> (firstly) demonstrates conclusively that if teachers change their practice from x to y there will be significant and enduring improvement in teaching and learning; and (secondly) has developed an effective method of convincing teachers of the benefits of, and means to, changing from x to y.
>
> (Hargreaves 1996: 5)

If it is to realize its commendable aims of school effectiveness and school improvement, research as portrayed here, demands 'objectivity', experiments and statistical proofs. There is a problem with this requirement though and the essence of it is that educational institutions and the individuals who are involved in and with them are a heterogeneous bunch with different attributes, abilities, aptitudes, aims, values, perspectives, needs and so on. Furthermore these institutions and individuals are located within complex social contexts with all the implications and influences that this entails. On its own, research whose findings can be expressed in mathematical terms is unlikely to be sophisticated enough to sufficiently accommodate and account for the myriad differences that are involved. As one group of prominent educational researchers have noted:

We will argue that schooling does have its troubles. However, we maintain that the analysis of the nature and location of these troubles by the school effectiveness research literature, and in turn those writing Department for Employment and Education policy off the back of this research, is oversimplified, misleading and thereby educationally and politically dangerous (notwithstanding claims of honourable intent).

(Slee *et al.* 1998: 1–9)

There is a need for rigorous research which does not ignore, but rather addresses, the complexity of the various aspects of schools and schooling: for research which explores and takes account of different objective experiences and subjective perspectives, and which acknowledges that qualitative information is essential, both in its own right and also in order to make full and proper use of quantitative indicators. The *Doing Qualitative Research in Educational Settings* series of books is based on this fundamental belief. Thus the overall aims of the series are: to illustrate the potential that particular qualitative approaches have for research in educational settings, and to consider some of the practicalities involved and issues that are raised when doing qualitative research so that readers will feel equipped to embark on research of their own.

At this point it is worth noting that qualitative research is difficult to define as it means different things at different times and in different contexts. Having said this Denzin and Lincoln's (1994) generic definition offers a useful starting point:

Qualitative research is multimethod in focus, involving an interpretive, naturalistic approach to its subject matter. This means that qualitative researchers study things in their natural settings, attempting to make sense of, or interpret, phenomena in terms of the meanings people bring to them. Qualitative research involves the studied use and collection of a variety of empirical materials . . . that describe routine and problematic moments and meanings in individuals' lives. Accordingly, qualitative researchers deploy a wide range of interconnected methods, hoping always to get a better fix on the subject matter at hand.

(Denzin and Lincoln 1994: 2)

The authors contributing to the series are established, well-known researchers with a wealth of experience on which to draw and all make use of specific and vivid examples from their own and others' work. A consequence of this use of examples is the way in which each writer conveys a sense of research being an intensely satisfying and enjoyable activity, in spite of the specific difficulties that are sometimes encountered.

Whilst they differ in terms of structure and layout each book deals with:

- The historical background of the approach: how it developed; examples of its use; implications for its use at the present time.

- Epistemological issues: the nature of the data produced; the roles of the researcher and the researched.
- Appropriate uses: in what research contexts and for which research questions is the approach most appropriate; where might the research be inappropriate or unlikely to yield the best data.

They then describe it and discuss using the approach in educational settings, looking at such matters as:

- How to do it: designing and setting up the research; planning and preparation; negotiating access; likely problems; technical details; recording of data.
- Ethical considerations: the roles of and the relationship between the researcher and the researched; ownership of data; issues of honesty.
- Data analysis.
- Presentation of findings: issues to do with writing up and presenting findings.

Michael Bassey's book, *Case Study Research in Educational Settings* engages with the criticisms made by Hargreaves (1996: 2) and by Tooley and Darby (1998) to the effect that much educational research is individualistic and does not contribute to cumulative body of knowledge. As an antidote to such research, Michael advocates the use of educational case studies as a prime strategy for developing theory which illuminates educational policy and enhances educational practice. Case studies are, of course, studies of singularities and so the suggestion that findings from them may be applied more widely may seem somewhat contradictory, if not invalid. The notion of 'fuzzy generalizations', or even more tentative, 'fuzzy propositions' which suggest that, for example, *it is possible* or *it may be in some cases* or *it is unlikely* is offered as a useful way forward. It is argued that, in any case, qualitative 'fuzzy generalizations' are more honest and more appropriate to much research in educational settings than are definitive claims for generalizability because of the complexity that is usually involved. In other words, in schools, doing *x* rarely invariably results in *y*.

Case Study Research in Educational Settings makes extensive use of examples of research projects which illustrate, vividly, the various potentials of the approach as well as demonstrating the practicalities involved in setting up and executing case study work. Anyone thinking of undertaking a case study will find it a useful source as will those concerned to argue that the study of specific situations has an important contribution to make to the development of educational theory, policy and practice.

Final note

It was Barry Troyna who initially came up with the idea for this series. Although his publishing career was extensive, Barry had never been a series editor and, in his inimitable way, was very keen to become one. Whilst he was probably best known for his work in the field of 'race', Barry was getting increasingly interested in issues to do with methodology when he became ill with the cancer which was eventually to kill him. It was during the twelve months of his illness that he and I drew up a proposal and approached potential authors. All of us knew that it was very likely that he would not live to see the series in print but he was adamant that it should go ahead, nonetheless. The series is, therefore, something of a memorial to him and royalties from it will be going to the Radiotherapy Unit at the Walsgrave Hospital in Coventry.

Pat Sikes

References

Denzin, N. and Lincoln, Y. (1994) Introduction: entering the field of qualitative research. In N. Denzin and Y. Lincoln (eds) *Handbook of Qualitative Research*. California: Sage.

Hargreaves, D. (1996) Teaching as a research-based profession: possibilities and prospects. Teacher Training Agency Annual Lecture. London: TTA.

Slee, R. and Weiner, G. with Tomlinson, S. (eds) (1998) Introduction: school effectiveness for whom? In *School Effectiveness for Whom? Challenges to the School Effectiveness and School Improvement Movements*. London: Falmer.

Tooley, J. and Darby, D. (1998) *Educational Research: A Critique – A Survey of Published Educational Research*. London: Ofsted.

Troyna, B. (1994) Blind faith? Empowerment and educational research, *International Studies in the Sociology of Education*, 4(1): 3–24.

Preface

This book is offered to all who set out to conduct educational research by case study. It gives new insights into case study as a tool of educational research. It suggests how case study can be a prime research strategy for developing educational theory which illuminates policy and enhances practice. It combines ideas from the literature with my experience over the past 25 years and puts forward a coherent view of what educational case study can be.

Several different kinds of educational case study are identified: theory-seeking, theory-testing, story-telling, picture-drawing, and evaluative case study; there are substantial examples of these. The book develops my recent advocacy of fuzzy generalization.

A stage-by-stage approach to conducting case study research includes an account of data collection and data analysis methods which is underpinned by concepts of trustworthiness and respect for persons. Structured, narrative and descriptive approaches to writing case study reports are featured with the idea of audit.

Many people have contributed through their own writings to the development of this book, but my special thanks are due to Dr Chris Holligan for allowing me to reconstruct a published case study of his, to Helen Morgan for allowing me to use a case study of hers, to Mrs M, Mrs W and Mr A for the case studies of their classrooms which feature in Chapter 9 and to Sheila Hall who worked with me on the case study reported in Chapter 10.

Michael Bassey
Kirklington

Part I | Reconstruction of educational case study

1 | Why educational case study should be reconstructed

The aim of this book is ambitious: it is to reconstruct the concept of educational case study as a prime strategy for developing educational theory which illuminates educational policy and enhances educational practice. I set out to do this by identifying and focusing on a particular form of educational case study, which I am calling 'theory-seeking and theory-testing case study'. This I see as contributing to theory through 'fuzzy' generalizations. In addition, I conceive of other categories of educational case study: story-telling and picture-drawing case study, and evaluative case study. Figure 1.1 gives an overview of empirical educational research and tries to put the four major types of such enquiry – case studies, experiments, surveys and action researches – into perspective.

Properly the reader must ask, from what experience and on what authority is such a project launched? Three strands of my experience are described below which may make clear why such a venture is desirable. First is an account of my experience as an external examiner of dissertations and theses; second is an account of two overviews of research in the public domain in the UK gained through involvement in the universities' Research Assessment Exercises; third is an overview of some of my own writing on the problem of generalization over nearly twenty years. The only authority that I claim is in the extent to which my peers in the educational research community will judge the ideas worthwhile and choose to adopt them.

In order to establish straight away what a theory-seeking case study can look like, Chapter 2 provides an example. It is adapted from a research paper by Chris Holligan, which originally was published in the *British Educational Research Journal*, and is reconstructed here with his kind permission.

Chapter 3 gives an account of what others have said about case study and Chapter 4 locates educational case study on the map of research in education. This is followed by an account of how research could be disseminated through 'fuzzy' generalization and professional discourse in Chapter 5. Having read that far, I hope the reader will understand why I have felt it

Figure 1.1 An overview of empirical educational research

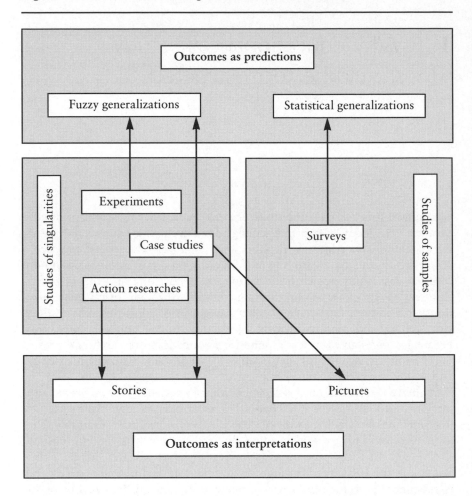

This overview suggests that there are two kinds of outcome of empirical educational research: predictions of what may happen in particular circumstances, and interpretations of what has happened in particular situations. It suggests that there are two kinds of arena for educational research, so that there are studies of singularities and studies of samples. The former embraces experiments, action researches and case studies; the latter surveys. Predictions may be statistical generalizations, where a quantitative estimate of the likelihood of something happening can be made (for example, 'there is a 50 per cent chance that . . .') or fuzzy generalizations, where a qualitative estimate only can be made (for example, 'it is very likely that . . .'). Interpretations may be written as stories (narrative-analytical accounts) or pictures (descriptive-analytical accounts). The idea is developed in this book that case study may lead to fuzzy generalization, story or picture.

desirable to 'reconstruct' the concept of case study – as set out in Chapter 6 – and perhaps will share my view of how case study should be delineated. If so then Chapter 7 provides a useful conclusion by suggesting ways in which educational case study may be conducted.

Part II consists of three substantial case studies which illustrate the various categories.

My experience as an examiner of master's dissertations and doctoral theses

I have been privileged over the past 25 years to examine well over a hundred dissertations and theses written by teachers on part-time master's courses and students taking PhDs. Each of these has been a study of a singularity, i.e. research into particular events rather than general events, this being virtually the only form of research open to people who are working at it part-time and with very limited resources. Some have called their work 'case study'.

Nearly all these dissertations have included empirical study of something professionally relevant to their authors. Some have been theoretical explorations of their own school or classroom practice, some evaluations of ongoing work and some action research into what is judged to be worthwhile change. Sometimes the teachers have attempted too much and have been unsuccessful in saying something significant, but usually they have come up with findings that are of consequence in the context of their school and pertinent to their work. Sometimes there is evidence that these findings have been shared with colleagues. Only occasionally do the findings get beyond the university library shelf, by being published in journal articles.

Invariably it has been for the author an *opus magnum*, a venture which for a period of time has taken over every spare hour: this is often acknowledged in the form 'with loving thanks to my dear spouse and children whom I have neglected while this has been written'. Frequently there seems to be a hidden message of 'never again'. Constructed with painstaking diligence, the dissertation represents in an academic sense the author's 'finest hour'. Chapter after chapter has been agonized over to get a worthwhile structure and to try to communicate meaning effectively; page after page has been carefully phrased and accurately referenced, with typographic errors eliminated. In this tutors have also played a supportive and demanding role. Only rarely have I found it necessary to refer the work back for revision of the text.

There are no nationally agreed criteria for what constitutes a 'pass' in the examination of a dissertation or thesis in education, but there is a broad consensus as to what is required. The study should focus on some educational issue or problem; the context and the methodology should be discussed with appropriate reference to the academic literature; the collection, analysis and interpretation of data should be trustworthy and ethical; the conclusions should not generalize beyond the empirical evidence, other than, where appropriate, to augment existing claims in the literature; there should be an abstract which summarizes the claim to knowledge; and the whole should be presented neatly, grammatically, in accord with academic conventions and without typographic errors. Most candidates who submit a dissertation achieve sufficiently well in terms of these expectations that they pass and are awarded the degree.

Looking back, I have a sense of disquiet. While some of the dissertations that I have seen have been 'a good read' with valuable insights into some educational practice, too many others have the marks of ritual, as though the writing of a dissertation is seen as no more than an initiation ceremony.

One problem is the obsessive use of the literature. I have written elsewhere (Bassey 1992: 14; 1995: 77) of genuflection (ritualistic citing of the founding parents of theory), sandbagging (adding to a statement inert defences – in the form of unqualified literature citations – to make it look secure) and kingmaking (giving undue authority to someone by citing unresearched utterances). These are fripperies in writing style designed to impress the innocent reader by the extent of the references cited. The academic world should long ago have abandoned this pretentiousness and learned to restrict citation to those studies which impinge directly on the work in hand. The best researchers certainly do this – but regrettably I find students are still being trained in the bad old habits!

A second problem is over-personalizing the account of research. I find a tendency for dissertation writers, in giving a narrative account of their work (which I applaud), to give too much detail. Do we really need to know that 'At this stage of my work I thought it would be helpful to see what the literature had to offer so I went to the university library'. In case study work it is important to give personal details that may have relevance to the findings, but statements like the above look like padding to help reach the expected quota of words.

But the third problem is the worrying one. An enormous amount of time and intellectual effort is vested in researching for and writing the dissertation. Other than giving a qualification to its author, what is achieved? Here there is perhaps a difference between the writing produced for a doctorate and for a master's degree. The doctorate is often a key step in the career development of a researcher and a short version of the thesis is frequently published in the academic literature. My guess is that most PhD students go on to do more research – as contract researchers or as university lecturers. However, there are few who take doctorates and many who pursue master's courses. The majority of people taking a master's are school teachers and the sad impression is that few of them, having gone through the initiation, subsequently engage further in research. Likewise, as mentioned above, few of their studies are published and so move into the public domain for other teachers to read and reflect on. The time and effort expended is not taken further. That is not to say that it has been wasted, for much will have been learned through the process, but it doesn't achieve its potential.

Let me state clearly that I believe that the outcome of a master's course should be twofold. First, it should have changed a teacher into one who, as time and opportunity arises, reads research reports critically and carries out research enquiries on issues related to his or her educational practice. (Or, if this was happening before studying for the master's qualification, afterwards it should be happening with greater effectiveness.) Second, the dissertation should have led to a short paper in the public domain which makes a claim to knowledge and which could be of consequence to other teachers.

This brings me to the second starting point for this book: concern about what is achieved by research published in the public domain.

My experience of research in the public domain

In 1992 and again in 1996 I was a panel member in the Higher Education Funding Councils' (of the UK) Research Assessment Exercise (RAE). With a dozen colleagues I was party to judging the quality of research coming from about a hundred departments of education in UK universities and colleges. In 1996 this meant having an overview of some 10,000 papers and books published during the previous four years in education. This is not the place to argue that we had an impossible task: we accomplished it to the best of our ability and the outcomes have already determined the research funding of the departments concerned. What is important here is to determine what insight it gives to the vexed question of how effective current educational research in the UK is in developing theory which illuminates policy and enhances practice.

After the exercise was complete, and with the support of the British Educational Research Association (BERA), Hilary Constable and I analysed the documents into fields of study. The allocations were based on title, with orientation of journal sometimes being an aid in the case of journal papers. The results of our analysis were published in BERA's newsletter, *Research Intelligence*, in July 1997 (Bassey and Constable 1997: 6–8).

Table 1.1 gives the sorting frame of categories and fields of enquiry which we used. The 41 fields of enquiry were identified 'in conversation with the data' and were placed into eight categories which were felt to have some semblance of educational logic. Three miscellaneous fields had to be added to embrace papers which could not be fitted in elsewhere. The problem of a paper straddling more than one field was handled using a hierarchic principle in an attempt to reduce arbitrariness. Where a publication fell into more than one category, allocation was made – if possible – into the field which seemed to be the most prominent. Where this couldn't be determined (as was often the case), the allocation was made to the field of enquiry with the lowest key

Table 1.1 RAE analysis: sorting frame of fields of educational research

Curriculum issues
1 Art education
2 Design and technology education
3 English education including reading, writing, oracy, literacy etc.
4 Geography education
5 History education
6 IT education
7 Languages (other than English) education: modern languages, classical languages
8 Mathematics education
9 Music education
10 Physical education
11 Science education
12 Environmental education
13 Health education
14 Personal, social, moral education
15 Religious education

School/teacher/child issues
16 School management, effectiveness, improvement; school development planning
17 Classroom management
18 Teacher issues: life-histories, career structures, workload, stress
19 Equal opportunities, gender, ethnic issues
20 Special educational needs

Teaching/learning issues
21 Pedagogy in general (not specific to a subject)
22 Assessment in general (not specific to a subject)
23 Curriculum in general (not specific to a subject)

Governance
24 Governance – school governors, LMS, school finance, GM
25 Macro educational policy – national government, LEAs

Phase areas
26 Nursery education (i.e. under 5 years)
27 Primary education (include KS1, KS2, infant, junior)
28 Secondary education (include KS3, KS4)
29 Post-compulsory education (i.e. post-16 but not obviously FE or Higher)
30 Higher education
31 Further education, vocational education, NVQ etc.
32 Adult education, continuing education, life-long education
33 Teacher education – ITT
34 Teacher education – INSET; professional development of teachers
35 Other professions' education (nursing, police, agriculture)

Overseas studies
36[*] Overseas studies – policy or practice

Disciplines in educational settings
37[*] History of education
38 Philosophy of education
39 Sociological theory developed from educational settings
40 Psychological theory developed from educational settings

Methodology
41 Research methodology

Other papers
42 Other
X Unclassified – impossible to decide
Y Seems not to be educational research in any recognizable form

Reference: Bassey and Constable (1997: 6)

number in the sorting frame. Thus a paper about the classroom management of art classes in primary schools would be listed under (1) rather than under (17) or (27) and a book about assessing mathematics at Key Stage 3 would be listed under (8) rather than (28). There were two exceptions to this rule, marked with an asterisk. 'Overseas education' (item 36) and 'History of education' (item 37) took precedence. Thus the classroom management of art classes in primary schools in France would go under (36) and science education in the nineteenth century would go under (37).

The outcome of this analysis is shown in Table 1.2. The eight categories are in the same rank order as on the sorting frame, but within each category the fields of enquiry have been ranked according to the number of publications allocated to them. It is important to bear in mind the hierarchic procedure which was used and to see this listing as no more than a very crude account of the educational research that surfaced as esteemed publications from UK higher education institutions in the period 1992–6.

This would be a very impressive table if there was a general view that educational research was making a significant impact on policy and practice. But there is not. We may ask what effect the 857 papers in the curriculum field of English have had. How has the teaching of mathematics been influenced by the publication of 565 papers investigating it? What has been the impact on the teaching of art, or geography or history – or any other of the subjects listed? What have school managers learned from the 321 papers published in their field? What has the government learned from the 282 papers in the field listed as macro educational policy? Of the 685 papers published on initial teacher education (ITT), how many have influenced the practice of ITT or the views of the Teacher Training Agency? These are, of course, rhetorical questions, for no one knows the answers. But the impression is that the impact of this enormous amount of research has been slight. When the Chief Inspector of Schools and others make trenchant attacks on educational research (as happened in 1997), the research community fights back with a strong sense of injustice but with frail weapons.

After the previous RAE I carried out a much smaller exercise than the one reported above and concluded:

> although there are some significant insights, overall the individualism and isolation of many of these researchers is unhelpful. There is too often a prevailing dilettante tradition of individual enquiry which looks like a game of trivial pursuits.
>
> There is certainly some outstanding work giving significant insights, for example in constructivist learning, pupil assessment, school effectiveness, science education, and equal opportunities, but beyond this I am less certain that much of the research reported in the literature appreciably extends theory, or illuminates policy, or improves practice, in significant ways. I have a strong impression of individualism, of

researchers working in isolation from each other, dabbling in a rather amateurish way at issues which are too big to be tackled by lone researchers.

(Bassey 1995: 127–8)

After the 1996 exercise, I have a longer list of significant insights and see a

Table 1.2 RAE analysis: crude summary of esteemed educational research coming from UK HEIs in the period 1992–1996

Curriculum issues	**3496**	*Phase areas*	**2724**
English	857	Initial teacher education ITT	685
Mathematics	565	Higher education	673
Science	523	Other professions' education	393
Religious Education	165	INSET	237
Design & Technology	150	Further education	229
Languages other than English	148	Adult education	217
Art	146	Primary education	126
History	145	Nursery education	73
Geography	137	Post-comp education	60
Information Technology	130	Secondary education	31
Physical Education	127		
Music	115	*Overseas studies*[*]	**788**
Environment	113		
Health	93	*Disciplines in educational settings*	**759**
Personal & Social Education	82	Psychology of education	237
		Sociology of education	214
School/teacher/child issues	**1297**	History of education[*]	199
Special educational needs	448	Philosophy of education	109
School management	321		
Equal opportunities	320	*Research methodology*	**137**
Teacher issues	129		
Classroom management	79	*Other papers*	**1174**
		Not educational papers	540
Teaching/learning issues	**826**	Categories not listed above	340
Pedagogy	408	Unclassifiable by title	294
Curriculum	215		
Assessment	203	*Total*	**11613**
Governance	**412**		
Macro educational policy	282		
Governance of schools	130		

Note: constituent items are given under the headings, thus English 857 is part of Curriculum issues 3496. Numbers represent publications – articles, books, occasionally conference papers
Source: Bassey and Constable 1997: 6–8

reduction in trivial pursuits, but still have major concerns about the lack of overall coherence of much of the work.

Many of these publications are in the empirical realm, i.e. based on first-hand collection of data, and inevitably the scale of enquiry is limited to small numbers of children, teachers, schools etc. If they had been conducted according to the approach that I am advocating in this book, they would have provided an array of fuzzy propositions and generalizations which could have contributed to the coherence which I believe is needed.

David Hargreaves, Professor of Education of the University of Cambridge, giving the annual Teacher Training Agency lecture in 1996, said:

> Much educational research is . . . non-cumulative, in part because few researchers seek to create a body of knowledge which is then tested, extended or replaced in some systematic way. A few small-scale investigations of an issue which are never followed up inevitably produce inconclusive and contestable findings of little practical relevance. Replications, which are more necessary in the social than the natural sciences because of the importance of contextual and cultural variations, are astonishingly rare . . . Given the huge amounts of educational research conducted over the last fifty years or more, there are few areas which have yielded a corpus of research evidence regarded as scientifically sound and as a worthwhile resource to guide professional action.
>
> (Hargreaves 1996: 2)

In this respect I agree with Hargreaves, but, as I shall argue later, his call for research which 'demonstrates conclusively that if teachers change their practice from x to y there will be a significant and enduring improvement in teaching and learning' (Hargreaves 1996: 5) ignores the complexity of educational settings and so is unhelpful in this form. However, it provides a starting point for rethinking the nature of educational case study.

My writing and thinking about research

I find that writing is a wonderful stimulus to thought. I am a messy writer for whom the cut-and-paste facility of word processors is a god-send compared to the scribble-scissors-and-glue which I used to use. My ideas jerk rather than flow down the screen; until I start writing I am not sure to where they will lead and consequently there are many false starts and deleted chunks of text. There are also long periods of time when nothing happens and then I come back to earlier writings and find new insights.

I have been writing about generalization and case study since 1980. Revisiting some of the papers from that time (Bassey 1980, 1981, 1983), I now think I was over-harsh in my rejection of generalization as a worthwhile ambition for studies of singularities. This is not to deny the validity of the attacks I made on those whom I found guilty of drawing unqualified generalizations from relatively small-scale studies. These arguments were brought together and elaborated in *Creating Education through Research* (Bassey 1995: Chapters 6 and 7) and still stand in my view. But I failed to recognize the potential value of what I shall now call a *fuzzy generalization*. This is the kind of statement which makes no absolute claim to knowledge, but hedges its claim with uncertainties. It arises when the empirical finding of a piece of research, such as

In *this* case it *has been* found that . . .

is turned into a qualified general statement like this:

In *some* cases it *may be* found that . . .

There is an academic literature of 'fuzzy logic'. In particular, Fourali (1997) has brought the term into educational discussion by arguing for 'fuzzy assessment' and in that field shown the value of imprecision rather than phoney exactness.

Previously I had treated the concept of generalization (of the empirical kind, that is) as a statement that had to be absolutely true. This is the sense in which physical scientists use the term. It is the basis of their concept of scientific method, as described by, say, Karl Popper (1963), in which a hypothesis stands as a generalization (or law) only if it withstands all attempts at refutation. I argued that there were very few generalizations (in this absolute sense) about education – and even fewer, if any, that were useful to experienced teachers. While still holding to this view in terms of scientific generalizations (i.e. the absolute kind), I now recognize that there are two other kinds of generalization which can apply in social science research: the statistical generalization and the fuzzy generalization. The statistical generalization arises from samples of populations and typically claims that *there is an x per cent or y per cent chance that* what was found in the sample will also be found throughout the population: it is a quantitative measure. The fuzzy generalization arises from studies of singularities and typically claims that *it is possible, or likely, or unlikely that* what was found in the singularity will be found in similar situations elsewhere: it is a qualitative measure.

A reconstruction of case study

In this book I am arguing that there are at least three categories of educational case study: theory-seeking and theory-testing case study; story-telling and picture-drawing case study; and evaluative case study. The first of these is a major concern, with the suggestion that the outcome of a theory-seeking or theory-testing case study should be a worthwhile and convincing argument supporting a fuzzy generalization (or in a more tentative form a fuzzy proposition). I believe that this idea could give coherence to many research endeavours in education and dispell the charge that educational researchers are engaged in trivial pursuits.

I hope to demonstrate clearly in this book how theory-seeking, theory-testing, story-telling, picture-drawing and (to a lesser extent) evaluative case studies can contribute to theoretical frameworks which underpin both educational practice and policy.

2 | An example of a theory-seeking case study leading to fuzzy propositions

It may be helpful to the reader at this early stage of the book to see an example of the kind of case study which can lead to fuzzy generalization. The following case report is based on an article by Dr Chris Holligan published in the *British Educational Research Journal*, 23(4), 533–50 (1997) and entitled 'Theory in initial teacher education: students' perspectives on its utility – a case study'. This version is abbreviated and rewritten to illustrate the concept of educational case study leading to fuzzy generalization as developed in this book; it is used with his kind permission. The report is followed by an 'audit certificate', which is an idea introduced in Chapter 7, and a checklist which checks whether the report meets the criteria of an educational case study, which are discussed in Chapter 6.

Theory in initial teacher education: some BEd students' perspectives on its utility in 1996 (Chris Holligan,[1] Open University)

Abstract

The evidence of this enquiry, arising from a study of 40 BEd students at Paisley University in 1996, and insofar as the teaching of Education Studies and grading procedures in other places can be related to those of the study, supports these two fuzzy propositions:

- BEd students are likely to perceive Education Studies as facilitating their teaching competence;
- BEd students who are graded as better teachers are likely to perceive more value in Education Studies than less able students.

The prime data source was two-hour semi-structured interviews with the students.

Introduction

This is a report of an enquiry into BEd students' perspectives on the utility of Education Studies in the Faculty of Education at Paisley University in 1996. It was funded by the Scottish Office Education and Industry Department and the School of Education of the Open University provided a grant to support it.

Conceptual background

Education Studies has always been an important element of initial teacher education (ITE). In this study it is seen as including academically oriented courses in developmental psychology, philosophical dimensions of education, curriculum models, educational research strategies and professional issues such as teacher appraisal. As taught at Paisley there is no sociology of education included.

Education Studies in ITE has had a chequered history. The James Report (1971) concluded that the theoretical study of education was largely irrelevant to students due to their lack of experience of working with pupils. Similarly, Her Majesty's Inspectorate (HMI) in 1979 in England and Wales found in their survey of college policies concerning Education Studies that the aim was to give students 'an analytic tool for considering educational issues', but found that most students were critical about its lack of 'immediate relevance' to the classroom, a finding in line with the Sneddon Report on ITE in Scotland of 1978 (Scottish Education Department 1978). Since then probably all ITE courses have striven to link Education Studies in college with experience in school, and this may explain the finding of the Office for Standards in Education (Ofsted) in 1992 that some two-thirds of newly qualified teachers viewed it favourably.

A number of academics have asserted the importance of Education Studies in ITE. For example, Goldstein (1986) claimed that an explicit understanding of the psychological foundations of learning is essential for effective teaching, Eraut (1989) argued that theoretical knowledge and understanding empowers students and that fostering theorizing should remain a core aim for higher education, and Furlong (1990) claimed that theoretical studies gives students opportunities to 'sort out their own fundamental values'.

It has become the topic of political polemic in which the New Right has claimed that Education Studies promotes subversive equalitarian ideals leading students to question traditional models of schooling in capitalist economies (O'Hear 1988; Lawlor 1990), leading to the view that theoretical studies of education are dispensable. However, according to a Labour Party (1991) policy statement about ITE, theory is a 'body of ideas which explains observed facts and phenomena' and its utility should be judged on the basis of how well courses provided by HEIs 'equip teachers to do their job': this is the stance of this paper.

Data collection

(a) Forty fourth-year BEd students preparing to teach in Scottish primary schools at the University of Paisley in 1996 were selected such that one cohort (A) had 20 students with high scores on school placements (mean score 93 per cent) and a second cohort (B) of 20 students had lower scores (mean score 65 per cent). The score for each student was the average of all classroom teaching grades (determined jointly by school and college staff) over the four years of the BEd. These students had already completed their final school placement.

(b) I interviewed each student for two hours (over two sessions) in an office on the university campus. The interviews were semi-structured explorations of their experience of aspects of the course and included this question (the answers to which are the focus of this paper): 'What does Education Studies help with?' With the permission of each student the interview was taped. Other issues explored are not reported in this paper.

I had taught some of the Education Studies courses to these students and so was known by them. Examination of the transcripts by some of my colleagues concluded that this did not invalidate the interview findings.

Data analysis I

The tapes were transcribed verbatim. The 40 responses to the question 'What does Education Studies help with?' were subjected to a content analysis of the transcripts and 18 categories of answers identified.[2] Four of these categories featured in the responses of 30 or more of the 40 students interviewed, viz. understanding children, professionalism in teaching, discipline in the classroom and differentiation of work in mixed ability classes. Examples of relevant data items from the interview transcripts are given below.

Understanding children   This comment is typical of how Education Studies was perceived by these students as stimulating further and deeper thought about issues.

> I'm aware of the general physical and cognitive aspects of development because I've seen it with my own children, but to actually focus and think about it and know why they do certain things and how developments affect each other . . . you knew children differed, but you weren't aware how much.

Professionalism in teaching   This is touched upon in many parts of Education Studies explicitly. Students gain a vocabulary, a sense of joining a community and of acquiring a set of standards which have to be adhered to. This is illustrated by these two data items:

You can talk to other professionals, other teachers on a similar level if they're talking in the staffroom, or if the teacher talks to you about a specific pupil and problems you're able to respond to that.

When I came in here I didn't know anything about how children think or what was expected of you as a teacher, your duties and responsibilities . . . if you want to be one of them these are the standards which you are going to have to meet. In my first year I wasn't professional, but I wanted to be.

Discipline in the classroom   An Education Studies course unit addressing psychological and practical aspects of discipline responded to this student's anxieties:

I was always frightened of how to deal with somebody in my class who was difficult . . . the course made me aware of the choices you have to deal with in a situation and the child's point of view as well as how your own teaching methods might create problems.

Differentiation with mixed ability classes   Coping with mixed ability classes is highlighted in the mentions given to differentiation; opportunities for discussing the issues in the Education Studies programme were valued, as this comment shows:

the special educational needs course was particularly helpful because we had the opportunity to discuss different kinds of educational difficulties which we'd come across in schools. You gain a far greater insight by discussing them with other people. It helps you to gauge children's levels and the teaching involved.

The ultimate judge of the utility of college theorizing is the personal experience of students, as this one said:

no matter how much you read a book or listen to a lecture you have to try it out yourself and I think it's the practical experience that helps put the theory into practice . . . school is real life, it gives opportunities to develop your own approach.

Data analysis II

This second analysis focuses on the four categories described above which featured in the responses of at least three-quarters of the students interviewed. They represent a high level of consensus in the chosen group of students. The numbers in the table are the number of interview data items coded by myself (and my research assistant) as coming in the category specified. Since one student might make more than one response in a category the numbers usually exceed 40. They were analysed between the two cohorts of students to see if there was a difference in their perceptions of Education Studies.

Responses from 40 BEd students to the question: What does Education Studies help with?

Four categories featured by more than 30 students in the two cohorts combined (ranked by number of responses from cohort A)	Responses from cohort A (n = 20 students with higher scores in school teaching)	Responses from cohort B (n = 20 students with lower scores in school teaching)
Understanding children	55	42
Discipline	43	23
Professionalism	41	36
Differentiation	32	27

Empirical findings and interpretation

The starting point of this enquiry was national concern about the value of Education Studies as taught to BEd students. Whereas university staff teaching the subject clearly see it as important for students, the focus of this research was how students see it, particularly in relation to their work in schools. The findings of this enquiry are that of these 40 BEd students at Paisley University in 1996, most perceived Education Studies as facilitating their teaching competence, with over three-quarters indicating that they had been specifically helped in the areas of understanding children, discipline, professionalism, and differentiation of work in mixed ability classes. In addition, the results given in the above table show that, in each of these four categories, those who were graded as better teachers on average perceived more value in Education Studies than, on average, did the less competent students. Whether Education Studies made them better teachers, or being better teachers made them more aware of what could be learned from Education Studies, is not clear; perhaps both occurred.

A reasonable interpretation of these findings is that the teaching of Education Studies to these students mattered: it was a valued part of their preparation for teaching. In terms of the Labour Party (1991) policy statement about ITE, this research gives evidence that the teaching of Education Studies helps to 'equip teachers to do their job' and suggests that the views of O'Hear (1988) and Lawlor (1990), that theoretical studies in education are dispensable, are ill-advised.

Fuzzy propositions

The evidence of this enquiry, insofar as the teaching of Education Studies and grading procedures elsewhere can be related to those of this study, supports these two propositions:

- BEd students are likely to perceive Education Studies as facilitating their teaching competence;
- BEd students who are graded as better teachers are likely to perceive more value in Education Studies than less able students.

It is hoped that others will follow up these propositions to test their trustworthiness.

References

Eraut, M. (1989) Initial teacher training and the NCVQ model. In J. W. Burke (ed.) *Competency Based Education and Training*. Lewes: Falmer.

Furlong, J. (1990) School based training: the students' views. In M. Booth, J. Furlong and M. Wilkin (eds) *Partnership in Initial Teacher Training*. London: Croom Helm.

Goldstein, H. (1986) Integration of theory and practice: a humanistic approach, *Social Work*, September/October, 352–6.

HMI (1979) *Developments in the BEd Degree Course: a Study Based on Fifteen Institutions*. London: HMSO.

James Committee (1971)*Teacher Education and Supply*. London: Department of Education and Science.

Labour Party (1991) *Investing in Quality: Labour's Plans to Reform Teacher Education and Training*. London: Labour Party.

Lawlor, S. (1990) *Teachers Mistaught: Training Theories or Education in Subjects?* London: Centre for Policy Studies.

Ofsted/HMI (1993) *The New Teacher in School: a Survey in England and Wales*. London: HMSO.

O'Hear, A. (1988) *Who Teaches the Teachers?* London: Social Affairs Unit.

Scottish Education Department (1978) *Learning to Teach: the Sneddon Report*. London: HMSO.

Audit certificate[3]

In terms of the evidence provided in this paper it is my professional judgement that the statement of empirical findings is based firmly on the data collected and that the enquiry has been conducted according to the ethical guidelines of respect for persons and respect for truth.

Signed: A. B. Smith, University of Barsetshire, 1 April 1996.

Replication invited[4]

The editors invite the submission of accounts of replications of this research. Such papers should be of no more than 1000 words and should treat the propositions put forward by the author as hypotheses to be tested in other settings. Replication papers need not include a conceptual background, but should focus on the research setting, any variations from the original method of enquiry (possibly a different methodology) and the findings. The conclusions should indicate whether the new research supports, amends or rejects the original propositions. Papers will be refereed, in accord with the standard practice of this journal, but the editors will endeavour to ensure rapid publication. Six issues from now publication of replications will cease and the original author will be invited to submit a review paper which considers whether the original propositions are sufficiently trustworthy to be described as fuzzy generalizations.

Claim that this enquiry meets the criteria of an educational case study[5]

(1)	What kind of an educational case study is this?	*A theory-seeking case study.*
(2)	Is this an empirical enquiry conducted within a localized boundary of space and time?	*Yes. 40 students, at Paisley in 1996.*
(3)	Does it examine *interesting* aspects of an educational activity, or programme, or institution, or system?	*Yes. Because of academic belief in the value of education studies as a training element for teachers, but right-wing political views that it is subversive and dispensable.*
(4)	Is it set mainly in its natural context and with an ethic of respect for persons?	*Yes. Students interviewed at the university and taped with their permission.*
(5)	Does it inform the judgements and decisions of practitioners, policy-makers, and/or theoreticians?	*Yes. Teacher education policy-makers.*
(6–12)	Were sufficient data collected for the researcher to be able . . .	*(40 students interviewed: each for two hours).*
(6)	. . . to explore *significant* features of the case?	*Yes.*
(7)	. . . to create *plausible* interpretations?	*Yes.*
(8)	. . . to test for the trustworthiness of these interpretations?	*Yes.*
(9)	. . . to construct a *worthwhile* argument or story?	*Yes. Leads to two fuzzy propositions.*
(10)	. . . to relate the argument to the literature?	*Yes.*

(11) ... to convey *convincingly* to an audience this argument or story?   *Yes. Tested out on two colleagues.*

(12) Is there a case record which could provide an audit trail that other researchers could use to validate or challenge the findings, or construct alternative arguments?   *Yes – in the author's possession.*

Notes

1 Now at the University of Paisley.
2 In the terminology used in Chapter 7 these categories, expressed in the form 'education studies helps with understanding children', were analytical statements.
3 The concept of an 'audit certificate' is discussed in Chapter 7. It is envisaged as an indication of probity requested by the author from a professional peer. In the journal literature it would precede a referee's comments; in the grey literature it would be the only measure of probity.
4 This also is discussed in Chapter 7. It is an attempt to establish a mechanism for obtaining and valuing replication studies which journals could adopt.
5 It is unlikely that journals would publish such claims, but they provide a useful checklist for author, 'auditor' and referee. The checklist arises from ideas developed in Chapter 6. Students are strongly recommended to use this approach in their dissertations.

3 | What is case study?

> While the literature is replete with references to case studies and with
> examples of case study reports, there seems to be little agreement about
> what a case study is.
>
> (Lincoln and Guba 1985: 360)

'What is case study?' is a good example of a question easy to ask and difficult to answer. This chapter examines what various researchers have said
about it in recent years. It is not a coherent story but is important background for the reconstruction of the concept that I am putting forward in
Chapter 6.

Towards a science of the singular

In December 1975 an invitational conference was held at Cambridge, spon-
sored by the Nuffield Foundation, on 'Methods of case study in educational
research and evaluation'. Subsequently Helen Simons edited the conference
contributions into a book entitled *Towards a Science of the Singular* (1980).
She noted that:

> [case study] has antecedents in the disciplines of sociology, anthro-
> pology, history and psychology and the professions of law and medi-
> cine, each of which developed procedures for establishing the validity
> of case study for their respective purposes. But the use of case study in
> education has been comparatively recent; its specific relevance to edu-
> cation has not been explored to the same degree.
>
> (Simons 1980: 1)

Adelman *et al.* (1980: 47), reflecting on this conference, wrote:

> Over the last ten years there has emerged a tradition of educational
> research and evaluation whose procedures, methods and styles of
> reporting have come to be collected under the general rubric of 'case

study'. Although case studies have made a considerable contribution to the corpus of knowledge and practical wisdom about education, they are often regarded with suspicion and even hostility. Their general characteristics remain poorly understood and their potential under-developed.

The original hope of the conference had been to suggest the shape of a hand-book of principles, procedures and methods of case study in education, but this did not happen because at the conference, as Simons reported, it became clear that 'there was still a need to clarify the epistemological and theoreti-cal assumptions underlying case study in educational research and evalu-ation . . . Methods are not defining in case studies' (Simons 1980: 8).

Later in this chapter other references will be made to this conference – a significant event in the history of educational research – but here is the place to give some of the 'possible advantages of case study' that were listed by Adelman *et al.* (1980: 59–60):

(a) Case study data, paradoxically, is 'strong in reality' but difficult to organise. In contrast other research data is often 'weak in reality' but susceptible to ready organisation . . .

(b) Case studies allow generalisations either about an instance or from an instance to a class. Their peculiar strength lies in their attention to the subtlety and complexity of the case in its own right.

(c) Case studies recognise the complexity and 'embeddedness' of social truths. By carefully attending to social situations, case studies can represent something of the discrepancies or conflicts between the viewpoints held by participants. The best case studies are capable of offering some support to alternative interpretations.

(d) Case studies, considered as products, may form an archive of descriptive material sufficiently rich to admit subsequent reinter-pretation . . .

(e) Case studies are 'a step to action'. They begin in a world of action and contribute to it. Their insights may be directly interpreted and put to use . . .

(f) Case studies present research or evaluation data in a more publicly accessible form than other kinds of research report, although this virtue is to some extent bought at the expense of their length.

Descriptions of case study given by different writers

Louis Cohen and Lawrence Manion first published their book *Research Methods in Education* in 1980. It has been reprinted many times and is now into its fourth edition: it is probably the widest used source book on research methods used by education students in the UK. In the third edition the authors devoted 30 of some 400 pages to a chapter on case studies. Their stance was this:

> Unlike the experimenter who manipulates variables to determine their causal significance or the surveyor who asks standardised questions of large, representative samples of individuals, the case study researcher typically observes the characteristics of an individual unit – a child, a clique, a class, a school or a community. The purpose of such observation is to probe deeply and to analyse intensively the multifarious phenomena that constitute the life cycle of the unit with a view to establishing generalisations about the wider population to which that unit belongs.
>
> (Cohen and Manion 1989: 124–5)

Five years earlier Barry MacDonald and Rob Walker, both at the Centre for Applied Research in Education (CARE) at the University of East Anglia, wrote a thought-provoking paper called 'Case-study and the social philosophy of educational research' (MacDonald and Walker 1975). They started with this definition:

> Case-study is the examination of an instance in action. The choice of the word 'instance' is significant in this definition, because it implies a goal of generalisation. We might say that case-study is that form of research where $n = 1$, only that would be misleading, because the case-study method lies outside the discourse of quantitative experimentalism that has dominated Anglo-American educational research.

They went on to hint at the paradox that recently Helen Simons has written about – and which ends this chapter. Having stated that educational case studies need the 'fusion of the styles of the artist and the scientist', they wrote: 'Case-study is the way of the artist, who achieves greatness when, through the portrayal of a single instance locked in time and circumstance, he communicates enduring truths about the human condition.'

At the Cambridge conference two definitions seem to have been favoured: 'the study of the instance in action' (as used by MacDonald and Walker) and 'study of a bounded system' (as used by Louis Smith). However, in a paper written after the experience of the conference, Stephen Kemmis (1980: 119) wrote:

> we must find a perspective on case study work which preserves indeterminacy, which countenances both the objects and methods of case study work, and which reminds us of the dialectical processes of its construction. If someone asked, 'what is the nature of case study as an activity?' then a proper response would be, '*Case study consists in the imagination of the case and the invention of the study.*'

Kemmis elaborated on the imagination of the case and the invention of the study in three powerful paragraphs that assert clearly the duties, responsibilities and opportunities of the case study worker. They deserve reproducing in full.

Such language might seem odd, but it makes explicit the cognitive and cultural aspects of case study research. It reminds us of the role of the researcher in the research: s/he is not an automaton shorn of human interests and programmed to execute a design devoid of socio-political consequences. It reminds us that knowledge is achieved through objectivisation: much as we may prefer to think otherwise, research is not a process of thought going out to embrace its object as if its object lay there inert, waiting to be discovered. And it reminds us of the active and interventive character of the research process: much as we may prefer to think otherwise, research is not merely the application of sophisticated techniques and procedures which yield up true statements as if we did not have to decide which techniques to use in which situations and how they must be modified to suit the particular conditions of any study.

The intertwined processes involved in the conceptualisation of a research problem, the investigation, the interpretation of findings and their application in the world beyond the study must be carried out with as much caution, rigour and compassion as the circumstances of each allow. In naturalistic research, these processes are especially 'visible': decisions about how they are realised in a study will very often affect life in the situation being studied. And often the decisions are taken 'on the spot', without the luxury of cool and considered reflection away from the real-life exigencies of the situation.

The imagination of the case and the invention of the study are cognitive and cultural processes; the case study worker's actions and his/her descriptions must be justified both in terms of the truth status of his/her findings and in terms of social accountability. Social science has the unique problem of treating others as objects for study; the unique problem in case study is in justifying to others why the researcher can be a knowledgeable observer-participant who tell what s/he sees.

(Kemmis 1980: 119–20)

Later in this chapter we will consider the issue of generalization arising from case study, but for the present it is noteworthy that not all commentators see it as an essential outcome. Lawrence Stenhouse, for example, writing the article on case study methods in the first edition of *Educational Research, Methodology and Measurement: an International Handbook,* was more concerned about producing case reports on which the reader could exercise judgement. He wrote:

Case study methods involve the collection and recording of data about a case or cases, and the preparation of a report or a presentation of the case . . . Sometimes, particularly in evaluation research, which is commissioned to evaluate a specific case, the case itself is regarded as of sufficient interest to merit investigation. However case study does not preclude an interest in generalisation, and many researchers seek theories that will penetrate the varying conditions of action, or applications founded on the comparison of case with case. Generalisation and application are matters of judgement rather than calculation, and the task of case study is to produce ordered reports of experience which invite judgement and offer evidence to which judgement can appeal.

(Stenhouse 1985: 49)

A decade later, in the second edition of this compendious handbook, the article on case study methods was written by Sturman, an Australian researcher with considerable experience of writing case studies. He focused attention on the holistic nature of cases and the need for the study of them to investigate the relationships between their component parts. He wrote:

'Case study' is a generic term for the investigation of an individual, group or phenomenon. While the techniques used in the investigation may be varied, and may include both qualitative and quantitative approaches, the distinguishing feature of case study is the belief that human systems develop a characteristic wholeness or integrity and are not simply a loose collection of traits. As a consequence of this belief, case study researchers hold that to understand a case, to explain why things happen as they do, and to generalise or predict from a single example requires an in-depth investigation of the interdependencies of parts and of the patterns that emerge.

(Sturman 1994: 61)

Robert Yin in the United States is probably the leading exponent in the social sciences of case study. He first published *Case Study Research: Design and Methods* in 1984; there were 13 additional printings and a second edition in 1994. In addition, in 1993 he published a companion volume entitled *Applications of Case Study Research*. In Yin's writings the essence of case study is that it is enquiry in a real-life context, as opposed to the contrived contexts of experiment or survey. He wrote that case study is

an empirical inquiry that:
- investigates a contemporary phenomenon within its real-life context, especially when
- the boundaries between phenomenon and context are not clearly evident.

He described this statement as a technical definition and added that a case study inquiry:

- copes with the technically distinctive situation in which there will be many more variables of interest than data points, and as one result

- relies on multiple sources of evidence, with data needing to converge in a triangulating fashion, and as another result
- benefits from the prior development of theoretical propositions to guide data collection and analysis.

(Yin 1994: 13)

Stake is another American researcher who has carried out many case studies and written extensively about them: in 1995 he brought together his ideas in *The Art of Case Study Research*. Whereas Yin's writing tends towards the positivist (or scientific) paradigm, Stake's is firmly within the interpretive paradigm. This is clearly shown by a footnote of his, which, in commenting on the difficulty of defining case study, says: 'conflicting precedents exist for any label. It is important for us to recognize that others will not use the words or the methods as we do' (Stake 1995: 2). How amazing that such a fundamental truth should be hidden away in a footnote!

Stake described case study as: 'the study of the particularity and complexity of a single case, coming to understand its activity within important circumstances' (p. xi). He elaborated on this in terms of a case having a boundary and of containing a coherent system:

> Louis Smith, one of the first educational ethnographers, helped define the case as 'a bounded system', drawing attention to it as an object rather than a process. Let us use the Greek symbol theta to represent the case, thinking all the while that theta has a boundary and working parts . . . The case is an integrated system. The parts do not have to be working well, the purposes may be irrational, but it is a system. Thus people and programs clearly are prospective cases. Events and processes fit the definition less well.
>
> (Stake 1995: 2)

Clearly the generic term 'case study' has a range of meanings: is this because there are different animals cohabiting in the same stable? Can we learn more by seeing how the above writers subdivide case study?

Types of case study described by various writers

Stenhouse (1985) identified 'four broad styles of case study': ethnographic, evaluative, educational and action research case studies. These deserve delineating here, although two of them (ethnographic and action research) are outside the scope of this book, being covered by other books in the series.

Of ethnographic studies, which he located within the social sciences, Stenhouse wrote:

> A single case is studied in depth by participant observation supported by interview, after the manner of cultural or social anthropology . . . Of ethnographic case study it may be said that it calls into question the

apparent understandings of the actors in the case and offers from the outsider's standpoint explanations that emphasise causal or structural patterns of which participants in the case are unaware. It does not generally relate directly to the practical needs of the actors in the case, though it may affect their perception and hence the tacit grounding of their actions.

(Stenhouse 1985: 49)

The other three 'broad styles' Stenhouse saw as concerned with different aspects of educational action. He described them in these terms:

In *evaluative case studies* a single case or collection of cases is studied in depth with the purpose of providing educational actors or decision makers (administrators, teachers, parents, pupils, etc.) with information that will help them to judge the merit and worth of policies, programmes or institutions.

Educational case study [is where] many researchers using case study methods are concerned neither with social theory nor with evaluative judgement, but rather with the understanding of educational action . . . They are concerned to enrich the thinking and discourse of educators either by the development of educational theory or by refinement of prudence through the systematic and reflective documentation of evidence.

Case study in action research . . . is concerned with contributing to the development of the case or cases under study by feedback of information which can guide revision and refinement of the action.

(Stenhouse 1985: 50)

It is worth at this point referring to a particular development in educational evaluation which dates from 1972. In that year Malcolm Parlett and David Hamilton, at the University of Edinburgh, began to circulate a paper entitled 'Evaluation as illumination: a new approach to the study of innovatory programmes'. It was not formally published until 1977 (Parlett and Hamilton 1977). They did not use the descriptor 'case study', but there can be no doubt that one form of evaluative case study is what they were about. They placed illuminative evaluation in what is now commonly called the interpretive paradigm (which they called the 'social anthropology paradigm'), and firmly rejected the positivist paradigm (which they called the 'agricultural-botany paradigm'). They gave this description.

The aims of illuminative evaluation are to study the innovatory programme: how it operates; how it is influenced by the various school situations in which it is applied; what those directly concerned regard as its advantages and disadvantages; and how students' intellectual tasks and academic experiences are most affected. It aims to discover and document what it is like to be participating in the scheme, whether

as teacher or pupil; and, in addition, to discern and discuss the inno-
vation's most significant features, recurring concomitants and critical
processes. In short, it seeks to address and to illuminate a complex array
of questions.

(Parlett and Hamilton 1977: 10)

This paper had an enormous impact on teacher researchers in the UK. I
remember getting a blurred photocopy of a photocopy of a photocopy in
1973. Many MEd students took it as a helpful model.

Sturman in his article in the second edition of Keeves's handbook was content to reiterate Stenhouse's four styles, but added a note that while ethnographic case study and action research case study are usually single site
studies, evaluative case study and educational case study may involve either
single or multiple sites.

Yin's categorization is in terms of three different forms of case study
which he labelled 'exploratory', 'explanatory' and 'descriptive'. His best
account of these is in the 1993 book:

An exploratory case study . . . is aimed at defining the questions and
hypotheses of a subsequent (not necessarily case) study . . . A descriptive case study presents a complete description of a phenomenon within
its context. An explanatory case study presents data bearing on cause-
effect relationships – explaining which causes produced which effects.

(Yin 1993: 5)

He extended the description of exploratory case study by including in it
attempts 'to discover theory by directly observing a social phenomenon in
its "raw" form' (ibid.), which he saw in terms of the grounded theory
approach of Glaser and Strauss (1967).

In the 1993 volume he devoted a chapter to case study 'as a tool for doing
evaluation', where 'evaluation is considered a particular type of research
intended to assess and explain the results of specific interventions' (p. 55).
He took a positivistic perspective and stated that case study, as an evaluation
method, 'assumes a single objective reality that can be investigated by
following the traditional rules of scientific inquiry' (p. 64).

Few evaluators in the UK would share his view that there is a 'single objective reality' to be investigated.

Stake (1995: 3) distinguished between intrinsic case study and instrumental case study. By intrinsic case study he referred to research into a particular situation for its own sake and irrespective of outside concerns: 'The
case is given. We are interested in it, not because studying it we learn about
other cases or about some general problem, but because we need to learn
about that particular case. We have an intrinsic interest in the case.' By instrumental case study, on the other hand, he referred to research into one or more
particular situations in order to try to understand an outside concern.

> We will have a research question, a puzzlement, a need for general understanding, and feel that we may get insight into the question by studying a particular case . . . This use of case study is to understand something else. Case study here is instrumental to accomplishing something other than understanding [the particular case] . . .

He went on to write: 'I am making the distinction . . . because the methods we will use will be different, depending upon intrinsic and instrumental interests' (p. 4). Stake used a second Greek letter – iota – to draw attention to the importance of issues.

> But what are issues? The word suggests that we face a problematic situation, even a sense of fulmination. Problems issue forth. Some problems are foci for our study. Issues are not simple and clean, but intricately wired to political, social, historical and especially personal contexts. All these meanings are important in studying cases. Issues draw us toward observing, even teasing out, the problems of the case, the conflictual outpourings, the complex backgrounds of human concern. Issues help us expand upon the moment, help us to see the instance in a more historical light, help us recognise the pervasive problems in human interaction. Issue questions or issue statements provide a powerful conceptual structure for organising the study of a case.
>
> (Stake 1995: 16–17)

Stake related the concept of issue to his two kinds of case study: 'One of the most important things to remember is that for intrinsic case study, theta is dominant; the case is of the highest importance. For instrumental case study, iota is dominant; we start and end with issues dominant' (p. 16).

Twenty years earlier, Adelman *et al.* (1980: 49) had reported a similar view after the 1975 Cambridge conference. (Since Stake was a participant he may have led this part of the discussion.) They wrote:

> Case study research always involves 'the study of an instance in action'. Yet lying behind the concept 'instance' lurk problems concerning the relationship of the 'instance' to the 'class' from which it is drawn. Case study research may be initially set up in one of two ways:
> (i) an issue or hypothesis is given, and a bounded system (the case) is selected as an instance drawn from a class . . .
> (ii) a 'bounded system' (the case) is given, within which issues are indicated, discovered or studied so that a tolerably full understanding of the case is possible.

How the problem of generalization is approached by different writers

The familiar criticism facing case study researchers is 'How can you generalize when $n = 1$?' We have seen that in Cohen and Manion's (1980) book establishing generalization about the population which the case represents is the aim of case study research, but for other writers it is not necessarily the endpoint and some see it as highly problematic.

Yin argued strongly for the importance of theory: 'For case studies, theory development as part of the design phase is essential, whether the ensuing case study's purpose is to develop or to test theory' (Yin 1994: 27). In terms of generalizing in order to create theory his book refers to 'statistical generalization' (which is unsuitable for case studies) and 'analytic generalization' (which can be appropriate). On the former he gave a firm warning: 'In statistical generalization, an inference is made about a population (or universe) on the basis of empirical data collected about a sample . . . a fatal flaw in doing case studies is to conceive of statistical generalization as the method of generalizing the results of the case' (Yin 1994: 30–1). This would seem to be exactly what Cohen and Manion were advocating! Yin argued that analytic generalization is the appropriate method for generating theory from case study, by which he meant that 'a previously developed theory is used as a template with which to compare the empirical results of the case study. If two or more cases are shown to support the same theory, replication may be claimed' (Yin 1994: 31).

Adelman *et al.* (1980: 50) recognized that 'generalization' might be an equivocal term and suggested that in relation to case study there are three kinds of generalization:

> The first kind is from the instance studied to the class it purports to represent (e.g. a study of comprehensivisation in one school may tell us about comprehensivisation in other schools). The second kind is from case-bound features of the instance to a multiplicity of classes (e.g. a study of comprehensivisation in one school may tell us about leadership or press reporting in other schools) [This is my example: MB.] Studies which do not begin by asserting the instance–class relation, however, will be inclined towards the third kind of generalisation: generalisations about the case.

Stenhouse, in his presidential address to the British Educational Research Association in 1979, with typical farsightedness described the coexistence of two 'cloven heads' in educational research. He said that he would 'try asserting' that 'the most important distinction in educational research at this moment is that between the study of samples and the study of cases' (Stenhouse 1980: 2).[1] He added: 'I believe that the description of cases and the analytic categorisation of samples are complementary and necessary approaches in educational research, and it is high time that the superficial stylistic differences between their proponents were recognised as impediments to good sense in the research community' (Stenhouse 1980: 4). He expected both to lead to generalization. He distinguished between predictive generalization and retrospective generalization. Predictive generalization is that which arises from the study of samples and is the form in which data are accumulated in the sciences: it is what Yin called 'statistical generalization'. Retrospective generalization is that which can arise from the analysis of case studies and is the form in which data are accumulated in history: in Yin's terms this is 'analytic generalization'. Stenhouse was concerned about teachers' classroom judgements and earlier had noted that, 'while predictive generalisations claim to supersede the need for individual judgement, retrospective generalisations seek to strengthen individual judgement where it cannot be superseded' (Stenhouse 1978).

Stake (1995: 7–8) expressed worries about generalization – 'Case study seems a poor basis for generalization . . . The real business of case study is particularization' – and then invented a new range of terminology about it. He suggested the term *petites généralisations* for general statements made within a study – for example that a particular child responds repeatedly in the same way to a particular situation. And he recognized that *grandes généralisations*, meaning general statements about issues of which the case is one example, can be modified by the findings of the particular case.

Instead of making *grandes généralisations*, Stake argued for researchers drawing from their research conclusions in the form of assertions (which later he called 'propositional generalizations'). 'Interpretation is a major part of all research . . . the function of the qualitative researcher during data gathering is clearly to maintain vigorous interpretation. On the basis of observations and other data, researchers draw their own conclusions. Erickson called them assertions, a form of generalization' (Stake 1995: 9). These assertions, he noted, will often be *petites généralisations* (i.e. located within the case study) but occasionally may refer to wider populations and so be *grandes généralisations*.

He went on to discuss how research data are interpreted in the form of assertions and reflected on how researchers may fail to make clear the speculative and tentative nature of their assertions.

> We do not have adequate guides for transforming observations into assertions – yet people regularly do it . . . The logical path to assertions often is apparent neither to reader nor to researchers themselves . . . For assertions, we draw from understandings deep within us, understandings whose derivation may be some hidden mix of personal experience, scholarship, assertions of other researchers. It will be helpful to the reader when such leaps to conclusions are labelled as speculation or theory, but researchers often do not.
>
> (Stake 1995: 9, 12)

Stake (1995: 12) was very gentle when he castigated fellow researchers for overstating their findings, but the importance of this paragraph is ignored at our peril:

> It is not uncommon for case study researchers to make assertions on a relatively small database, invoking the privilege and responsibility of

interpretation. To draw so much attention to interpretation may be a mistake, suggesting that case study work hastens to draw conclusions. Good case study is patient, reflective, willing to see another view of the case. An ethic of caution is not contradictory to an ethic of interpretation.

What beautiful language!

Stake introduced in 1982 (with Trumbull) the term 'naturalistic generalization'. By this they meant 'conclusions arrived at through personal engagement in life's affairs' (Stake 1995: 86). Here they were using the term 'generalization' to refer to the learning processes through which we individually acquire concepts and information and steadily generalize them to other situations as we learn more. Stake noted that Hamilton called this 'an inside-the-head generalization'. He also noted that naturalistic generalization can be made through 'vicarious experience [if it is] so well constructed that the person feels as if it happened to themselves' (Stake 1995: 86). It is the provision of this vicarious experience that he sees as a key role for case study writers.

> To assist the reader in making naturalistic generalizations, case researchers need to provide opportunity for vicarious experience. Our accounts need to be personal, describing the things of our sensory experiences, not failing to attend to the matters that personal curiosity dictates. A narrative account, a story, a chronological presentation, personalistic description, emphasis on time and place provide rich ingredients for vicarious experience.
>
> (Stake 1995: 87)

Stake contrasted these naturalistic generalizations, which are *made personally by the reader*, with the 'propositional generalizations' (or assertions) *made publicly by the researcher*. He urged case researchers to consider with care how much of their writing should provide input for the reader's naturalistic generalizations and how much should spell out the researcher's propositional generalizations. He recognized, of course, that the reader will do both, taking narrative descriptions to provide vicarious experience leading to naturalistic generalizations, and taking propositional generalizations (or assertions made by the researcher) alongside existing propositional knowledge to modify or extend it.

In 1985 an Australian researcher with considerable experience of classroom research, David Tripp, published a paper entitled 'Case study generalisation: an agenda for action'. His concern was with how research findings can be applied to classrooms by practising teachers and he argued for a cumulative process in bringing case studies together. He saw this as 'qualitative generalization' (what Stake called 'naturalistic generalization'), in which the individual, meeting the facts of a new case, applies them to his or her knowledge of similar cases, and so develops personal understanding. In order to do this Tripp argued that it is important for each case report to document carefully the salient features of the case. He suggested that there are two kinds of salient features: 'comparable' features (e.g. every classroom case study giving sex, age, ability and socio-economic status of the pupils, an account of the teaching facilities in the classroom and the teaching style of the teacher) and 'comprehensive' features (particular circumstances which are judged relevant to the events observed etc.). He then wrote: 'If several thousand case studies were in an archive, then the problem to emerge is how the studies could be made available so that a researched case appropriate to the needs of an inquirer may be found to illuminate an unresearched situation' (p. 37). Supposing that that were resolved by precise indexing of salient features and findings, Tripp then envisaged 'teachers with a particular problem first going to the archive to find how it occurs and has been dealt with elsewhere, then acting upon that vicarious experience in their own classrooms before finally documenting their experience to be added to the archive' (p. 41).

Academic criticisms of case study

Yin (1994: 9) recognized that within the academic community there is opposition to the idea of case study on the grounds of a 'lack of rigor' and 'little basis for scientific generalization', and 'they take too long and they result in massive, unreadable documents' (Yin 1994: 10). While refuting these accusations, he admitted that 'good case studies are very difficult to do' (Yin 1994: 11).

In 1985, two British long-term critics of some forms of case study research, Paul Atkinson and Sara Delamont, contributed to a book entitled *Educational Research: Principles, Policies and Practices*, which was edited by Marten Shipman. Describing themselves as 'committed practitioners of interpretive research methods, particularly ethnography' they launched a blistering attack on case study approaches to evaluation, in particular the illuminative evaluation of Parlett and Hamilton (1972). Their chapter was entitled 'Bread and dreams or bread and circuses? A critique of "case study" research in education'. First, to them it was 'remarkably difficult' to find anything like a definitive account of case study approaches to educational evaluation. They considered that 'the unit of analysis (case) can, in practice, mean just about anything' (p. 29), and later suggested that 'the case-study writers often seem in danger of reinventing the wheel: what is worse, they seem rather slapdash wheelwrights at that' (p. 32). Second, Atkinson and Delamont considered that case study evaluators (and in particular those at CARE at the University of East Anglia) had a deliberate commitment to an 'anti-intellectual or anti-academic tenor' (p. 34). They sensed a laudable intention 'to demystify the activities of research workers, to eliminate the sense of an elite and remote cadre of evaluation experts'

(p. 35), but argued that such a 'denial of theory and method is, we believe a denial of responsibility for one's research activities and conclusions' (p. 37). They also believed that among the case study researchers, 'a concern for ethics too often supplants equally important issues of theory and method' (p. 37). Third, Atkinson and Delamont noted that 'the proponents of case-study research often distinguish their enterprise from other research styles and approaches through a stress upon the unique, the particular, the "instance"' (p. 38). They argued that this approach to 'cases' is 'profoundly mistaken'. They were also concerned at the rejection of generalization, for 'if studies are not explicitly developed into more general frameworks, then they will be doomed to remain isolated one-off affairs, with no sense of cumulative knowledge or developing theoretical insight' (p. 39). They rejected Stake's concept of naturalistic generalization as expressed in his paper of 1980 on the grounds that by insisting on the supremacy of tacit, experiential and private knowledge, he confuses the way that a study is reported with the methodological principles by which the claim to knowledge is derived.

It might be expected that under this heading I would list Walker's 'Three good reasons for not doing case studies in curriculum research', the title of a paper he published in 1983. His concerns were that case study can be an uncontrolled intervention in the lives of others, can give a distorted view of the world and can have a tendency to embalm practices which are actually always changing. His paper is really about trying to minimize these dangers and for present purposes it is sufficient to draw attention to these three potential problems.

Endpiece

At this point the reader might expect me to summarize the various positions and terminology of the above writers into one coherent framework. I cannot. Perhaps Yin's concept of an 'analytic generalization' is very similar to Stenhouse's 'retrospective generalization', Erickson's 'assertion' and Stake's 'propositional generalization'. Perhaps Stake's 'intrinsic case study' is closely related to Parlett and Hamilton's 'illuminative evaluation', while these are poles apart from Yin's concept of evaluative case study. Perhaps Tripp's 'qualitative generalization' is akin to Stake's 'naturalistic generalization'. But to draw such comparisons is a dangerous game, for I cannot be sure that I have correctly elicited what these writers have meant by the terms they have used and, dare I say it, neither can we be sure that these writers themselves had clear, unambiguous concepts in their minds and managed to express them coherently. What I have tried to do is to highlight some of the published statements about case study research in education which have underpinned the writing of the following chapters.

I have left to the end a recent paper by Helen Simons entitled 'The paradox of case study' (1996). More elegantly than I, she reviews the development of case study research, mainly using different sources. Her emphasis is on educational evaluation, particularly in policy research. The importance of her paper is that she welcomes the paradox between the study of the singularity and the search for generalization.

> One of the advantages cited for case study research is its uniqueness, its capacity for understanding complexity in particular contexts. A corresponding disadvantage often cited is the difficulty of generalising from a single case. Such an observation assumes a polarity and stems from a particular view of research. Looked at differently, from within a holistic perspective and direct perception, there is no disjunction. What we have is a paradox, which if acknowledged and explored in depth, yields both unique and universal understanding.

> [We need to] embrace the paradoxes inherent in the people, events and sites we study and explore rather than try to resolve the tensions embedded in them . . . Paradox for me is the point of case study. Living with paradox is crucial to understanding. The tension between the study of the unique and the need to generalise is necessary to reveal both the *unique* and the *universal* and the *unity* of that understanding. To live with ambiguity, to challenge certainty, to creatively encounter, is to arrive, eventually, at 'seeing' anew.

> (Simons 1996: 225, 237–8)

In developing her argument she draws effectively on the use of paradox in painting and poetry and ends with lines from T. S. Eliot's *Four Quartets*:

> We shall not cease from exploration
> And the end of all our exploring
> Will be to arrive where we started
> And know the place for the first time.

Note

1 I have used this idea in Figure 1.1, but have interpeted it as the study of samples and the study of *singularities*.

4 | Locating educational case study on the map of research in education

In my book *Creating Education through Research* (1995) I sketched out a map of research in education which set out to demonstrate that it is 'a broad church' and embraces a wide range of intentions and purposes. For the purposes of the present book it is important to recognize that only part of the territory of 'research in education' is 'educational research', and only part of 'educational research' is 'educational case study'. I believe this delineation is most important if misunderstandings and paradigmatic feuds are to be avoided.

It will be helpful to reiterate some of the points made in *Creating Education through Research* here. First, I shall consider the concepts of 'education', 'research', 'educational research' and 'discipline research in educational settings'. Second, I shall consider the concept of 'empirical research' in education and its three categories of 'theoretical research', 'evaluative research' and 'action research'. Third, I shall look briefly at the two major paradigms of constructing reality – using the terms 'positivist' and 'interpretive'. Fourth, comes a discussion of scientific generalization and statistical generalization, in the context of the study of samples and then, finally, fuzzy generalization is introduced in the context of study of singularities and case study as a sub-set of these.

What is 'education'?

It is important for every researcher to be clear about what she or he means by education. In public discussion the concept of 'education' seems to be strangely located within the positivist paradigm, as though we all give it the same meaning. Thus Tony Blair, Prime Minister, announced in 1997 that his policy was 'Education, education, education': do we all give the same meaning to each of these three words?[1] Clearly not. For example, some see it as acquiring useful knowledge and skills in order to achieve a high quality of life, some as developing personally and socially as good people, and others as about creating wealth in order to increase the gross national product.

With trepidation, I set out a framework definition of education. It draws heavily on the writing of M. V. C. Jeffreys in a book entitled *Glaucon: an Enquiry into the Aims of Education* (1950), but also includes the concept of the 'worthwhile' used by R. S. Peters in *Ethics and Education* (1966).

Education is:

- first, the experience and nurture of personal and social development towards worthwhile living;
- second, the acquisition, development, transmission, conservation, discovery and renewal of worthwhile culture.

I call it a framework definition because it leaves open the meanings of 'worthwhile living' and 'worthwhile culture'. It embraces the activities of, for example, learners (experience, acquisition, development), teachers (nurture, development, transmission), scholars and librarians (conservation) and artists, scientists, engineers, politicians and researchers (discovery, development, renewal); but it does not embrace the individual meanings that they may give to the notions of worthwhile living and worthwhile culture. For example, the introduction of the National Curriculum in England and Wales, and its subsequent modifications, were massive attempts by government to define what shall be transmitted to children in schools as worthwhile culture. Likewise, the mission statements, pastoral policies and codes of behaviour which all schools in England and Wales were required to develop during the early 1990s were local definitions, devised by governors and teachers, of what constitutes, for them, worthwhile living.

What is research?

It is helpful to start from a general statement like this:

Research is systematic, critical and self-critical enquiry which aims to contribute to the advancement of knowledge and wisdom.

This, if accepted as a definition, provides a rational basis for arguments about whether, for example, case study is research. This is less of a problem than 20 years ago, but it is always useful to be able to say, 'If this case study is systematic, critical and self-critical enquiry which aims to contribute to the advancement of knowledge and wisdom, then it is research.'

What is educational research?

The logical approach is to couple together the above two definitions like this:

Educational research is systematic, critical and self-critical enquiry which aims to contribute to the advancement of knowledge and wisdom about the experience and nurture of personal and social development towards worthwhile living and the acquisition, development, transmission, conservation, discovery and renewal of worthwhile culture.

This is quite a mouthful and needs simplifying. The most important part of the beginning is the concept of critical enquiry. Thereafter it is significant that the key words 'experience', 'nurture', 'acquisition', 'development', 'transmission', 'conservation', 'discovery' and 'renewal' are all words involving someone in action – and entail that person engaging in judgements about what are worthwhile actions and making decisions about how to achieve worthwhile actions.

Thus the above can be expressed more succinctly as:

Educational research is critical enquiry aimed at informing educational judgements and decisions in order to improve educational action.

This is the kind of value-laden research that should have immediate relevance to teachers and policy-makers, and is itself educational because of its stated intention to 'inform'. It is the kind of research in education which is carried out by educationists.

But what of the various kinds of research that are concerned primarily with the *phenomena* of educational action and are not necessarily concerned with intentions to improve educational action? For example, sociologists, psychologists, anthropologists, economists, historians and philosophers conduct research in educational settings which contributes to theoretical knowledge about phenomena without necessarily focusing on informing the judgements and decisions of educational practitioners and policy-makers. These are different kinds of research from educational research as defined above, and I find it helpful to separate them.

What is discipline research in educational settings?

A general description of such research is:

Discipline research in education aims critically to inform understandings of phenomena pertinent to the discipline in educational settings.

The major audiences for such research will be respectively sociologists, psychologists, anthropologists, economists, historians and philosophers; but in addition teachers and policy-makers may find it relevant to their professional lives although not pertinent to their day-by-day decisions. In

Creating Education through Research (1995) I gave a number of examples to illustrate the validity of dividing research in educational settings in this way.

The distinction between educational research and discipline research in education is important for this book because it is about case study within educational research – and not within the various disciplines listed above. Thus ethnographic case study is not discussed in this book, nor psychological, historical or economic case study.

What is empirical research, and what are its categories?

Empirical research means the kind of research which focuses primarily on data collection. Not all research is like that: for example, *reflective research* entails systematic and critical enquiry into the writings of others and *creative research* is about systematic and critical enquiry leading to new systems, novel solutions to problems and unique artefacts. Empirical research is where questions are asked of people, observations made of events and descriptions taken of artefacts, by researchers who are using their senses to collect data and their intelligence to ensure that it is done systematically by trustworthy procedures, critically analysed and wisely interpreted, with fair conclusions drawn.

I find it helpful to identify three different categories of empirical research, which I describe as: *theoretical research*, which is enquiry carried out in order to understand; *evaluative research*, which is enquiry carried out in order to understand and evaluate; and *action research*, which is enquiry carried out in order to understand, evaluate and change. I believe these apply across a range of societal activities, but here we are concerned with them in educational research, i.e. in terms of enquiry that informs judgements and decisions aimed at improving educational action, and in particular in relation to educational case studies rather than in, for example, the study of educational samples.

Theoretical research as a subset of educational case study research: enquiry carried out in order to understand

This category of research work has the purpose of trying to describe, interpret or explain what is happening without making value judgements or trying to induce any change. The researchers are trying to portray the topic of their enquiry as it is. The aim is to give theoretical accounts of the topic – perhaps of its structures, or processes, or relationships – which link with existing theoretical ideas. They are not seeking to evaluate it and they strive to investigate without disturbing. Of course, others may use the findings to initiate change, but the researchers themselves aim to complete the enquiry without changing the situation.

Theory-seeking and theory-testing case studies (which are explained in Chapter 6) obviously come in this category, and some story-telling case studies do as well.

Evaluative research as a subset of educational case study research:
enquiry carried out in order to understand and to evaluate

This second category of research is work done by evaluators – and it needs to be clearly asserted that, provided the enquiry is conducted systematically and critically, evaluation is a branch of research. Like the theoreticians, the evaluators seek to understand what is happening within the case. They are trying to describe, interpret or explain what is happening, but in doing so they are setting out to make value judgements, or to portray events so that others may make value judgements, about the worthwhileness of the case. The expected endpoint is that someone will use their findings to decide whether or not to try to induce change.

Evaluative case study is one of the three kinds of educational case study identified in Chapter 6.

Action research as a subset of educational case study research:
enquiry carried out in order to understand, evaluate and change

A third category of educational research is carried out by action researchers. They are teachers or managers who are trying to make beneficial change within their own workplace. In order to do this it is first necessary to understand what is happening and to evaluate it, then to introduce change and evaluate the new situation. Action researchers are using systematic and critical enquiry in attempts to improve their practical situation.

Whereas successful theoretical research and evaluative research invariably lead to written reports in order to serve the research purpose of advancing knowledge and wisdom, successful action research is often recorded only in the memories of those who participated. They know, and are wiser because of knowing, what was the outcome of the change in their workplace – but the rest of the world may not be given the chance to share that understanding. In terms of the different types of educational case study described later, action research could always be recorded as a 'story-telling' case study and often might be written up as either a theory-seeking study or a theory-testing study.

Mobility between the categories

Referring to 'categories' of research work does not imply that there is no mobility between the categories, for obviously a researcher may act at one time as a theoretician, at another time as an evaluator and at another as an action researcher.

How do different beliefs in the nature of reality affect educational case study?

In striving to make sense of the world, researchers seem to work from different beliefs about the nature of reality. Of the various terms used to describe these beliefs I use the terms positivist paradigm and interpretive paradigm. (Students need to recognize that my drawing of this distinction and my attempts at using these terms are unlikely to be acceptable to all academics.) A research paradigm is a network of coherent ideas about the nature of the world and of the functions of researchers which, adhered to by a group of researchers, conditions the patterns of their thinking and underpins their research actions.

The positivist research paradigm

To the positivist there is a reality 'out there' in the world that exists whether it is observed or not and irrespective of who observes. This reality can be discovered by people observing with their senses. Discoveries about the reality of human actions can be expressed as factual statements – statements about people, about events and about relationships between them. To the positivist the entire world is rational, it should make sense and, given sufficient time and effort, it should be possible for it to be understood through patient research. The researcher can then explain the reality she or he has discovered to others, because language is an agreed symbolic system for describing reality.

Positivist researchers do not expect that they themselves are significant variables in their research; thus, in testing an hypothesis, they expect other researchers handling similar data to come to the same conclusion that they find. Because of this, positivists' preferred method of writing reports is to avoid personal pronouns. 'I' or 'me' is not considered relevant.

Because things and events are real irrespective of the observer, positivists have little difficulty in giving them descriptive labels. Thus labels like 'truant', 'deep and surface thinking' or 'local education authority', provided they are carefully defined, are not seen as problematic and so the possessors of these labels can be counted – the quantity can be measured – and subjected to statistical analysis. This is why the methodology of the positivists is often described as 'quantitative'.

The word 'positivist' is not always recognized by those who work within this paradigm and sometimes is used pejoratively by those engaged in alternative paradigms. In return it is sometimes the case that positivist researchers reject the idea of an interpretive paradigm being a valid basis for research.

To the positivist researcher the purpose of research is to advance knowledge by understanding and describing the phenomena of the world and sharing the findings with others. Understanding enables one to explain how particular events occur and how they are linked in a theoretical structure. It may provide predictions about future events.

The interpretive research paradigm

The interpretive researcher cannot accept the idea of there being a reality 'out there' which exists irrespective of people, for reality is seen as a construct of the human mind. People perceive and so construe the world in ways which are often *similar* but not necessarily the *same*. So there can be different understandings of what is real. Concepts of reality can vary from one person to another. Instead of reality being 'out there', it is the observers who are 'out there'. They are part of the world which they are observing and so, by observing, may change what they are trying to observe. The interpretive researcher considers that the rationality of one observer may not be the same as the rationality of another, and so accepts that when these two observers talk to each other the world may not seem 'rational' and 'make sense'. The interpretive researcher sees language as a *more or less* agreed symbolic system, in which different people may have some differences in their meanings; in consequence the sharing of accounts of what has been observed is always to some extent problematic. Because of differences in perception, in interpretation and in language it is not surprising that people have different views on what is real.

Interpretive researchers reject the positivists' view that the social world can be understood in terms of general statements about human actions. To them the descriptions of human actions are based on social meanings, people living together interpret the meanings of each other and these meanings change through social intercourse.

Interpretive researchers recognize that by asking questions or by observing they may change the situation which they are studying. They recognize themselves as potential variables in the enquiry and so, in writing reports, may use personal pronouns.

The data collected by interpretive researchers are usually verbal: fieldwork notes, diaries and transcripts and reports of conversations. Sometimes interpretive data can be analysed numerically but more usually they are not open to the quantitative statistical analysis used by positivists. They are usually richer, in a language sense, than positivist data and, perhaps because of this quality, the methodology of the interpretive researchers is described as 'qualitative'.

Phenomenology, ethnomethodology, hermeneutics and social anthropology are more or less alternative labels for the interpretive paradigm. Each has its own adherents, who no doubt challenge the simplicity of the previous sentence! Ethnography is a branch of this paradigm, concerned with participant observation – where the observer is not 'a fly on the wall', but becomes a participant in the activity which she or he is studying.

To the interpretive researcher the purpose of research is to advance knowledge by describing and interpreting the phenomena of the world in attempts to get shared meanings with others. Interpretation is a search for deep perspectives on particular events and for theoretical insights. It may offer possibilities, but no certainties, as to the outcome of future events.

Educational case study and the reality paradigms

The public world is positivist; the private world is interpretive. That is a bold statement, but one that I suggest is a reasonable approximation to the truth. Thus when the newspapers tell their readers about schools or teachers there are simple assumptions made that 'schools are where children go to learn' and 'the teacher's job is to teach children'. The problem for case study researchers is that when they unpick these simple positivist assumptions they find that concepts like 'school' and 'teacher' have a very wide range of meanings, which have very significant implications for practitioners and policymakers. The exploration of a particular case is essentially interpretive, in trying to elicit what different actors seem to be doing and think is happening, in trying to analyse and interpret the data collected (which may seem a lot, but are inevitably only a fraction of what could be collected) and in trying to make a coherent report which is long enough to be meaningful and short enough to be readable. Be warned – case study is difficult.

What are scientific, statistical and fuzzy generalizations?

When I wrote *Creating Education through Research* (1995) I drew a distinction between the search for generalizations and the study of singularities, which was based on earlier writing going back to 1981. As mentioned in Chapter 1, my understanding of these issues has developed since then by recognizing three different kinds of generalization arising from empirical study. There are scientific generalizations, statistical generalizations and fuzzy generalizations.

The *scientific generalization* is what the classical physicist looked for: if the voltage across a resistance is increased the current will increase in proportion (Ohm's law); if the pressure on a mass of gas (at constant temperature) is increased, the volume will decrease in a linear relationship (Boyle's law). As taught by Popper (1963), if an exception is found the scientific generalization must be rejected, or modified to encompass the circumstances of the exception. Unfortunately the language of classical physics crept into educational debate and so statements like these were made as the outcomes of substantial research studies: 'the lecture is as effective as other methods for transmitting information' and 'in reading, pupils of formal . . . teachers progress more than those of informal teachers' (cited in my 1981 paper). In certain circumstances these statements had been found to be true, but the implied generalization to all circumstances was nonsensical. Scientific generalization is not appropriate for summarizing social findings because of the sheer complexity of social events. A litre of oxygen in Hong Kong will have exactly the same properties as a litre of oxygen in New York, but the same cannot be expected of a classroom of children from each of these two cities – nor from two classrooms in the same city.

Classical physical scientists did not have to worry about samples. What was true in one laboratory would be true in any laboratory, at any time. Once a law of nature had been substantiated it could be used to predict phenomena elsewhere. In part this is because the litre of oxygen under atmospheric conditions, for example, contains millions of millions of molecules of oxygen, with as many moving to the right as to the left, and as many moving upwards as downwards, statistically speaking. But imagine a weightless jar containing just 10 molecules: one could calculate the statistical chance of all the molecules hitting one wall at the same time – and knocking the jar over! Classical physical science can make irrefutable generalizations because it is dealing with enormously large populations.

Social scientists have smaller populations and usually more variables to cope with, and so when they quantify their results have to use the concept of the *statistical generalization*. This expresses the chance that something will be the case. The best known educational example is probably the two thirds rule: two-thirds of the time in a classroom someone is talking, and during two-thirds of that time it is the teacher doing so. Gowin (1972) demolished this rule in these words:

> This regularity in educational phenomena has been consistently observed and recorded over decades. It looks like an empirical generalisation that will hold up like generalisations in chemistry or some other science. But change the educational concept from self-contained classrooms to open-learning centres, from group instruction to personalised instruction – change the education concepts which direct the educational practice and the regularity expressed in the two-thirds rule will vanish from the educational scene.

Statistical generalizations come from studies of samples. In 1998 Blatchford and Sumpner published the results of a questionnaire survey to which a random sample of 1245 teachers of English primary schools responded. One of the questions asked whether pupil behaviour out-of-school had changed over the last five years. Of their sample 55% said it had declined, 35% said 'no change', and 5% reckoned it had improved. This is not the place to discuss the methodology of sampling, other than to indicate that another random sample at the same time, of different teachers but drawn from the same population of primary school teachers in England at the same time, should give the same result if the two samples were effectively drawn. The

55–35–5 result is an empirical finding. On the assumption of valid sampling it could lead to a statistical generalization: the opinion of primary school teachers in England in 1996 on changes in pupil behaviour out-of-school over the previous five years was that 55% considered it had declined, 35% said 'not changed' and 5% said 'improved'. In other words the statistical generalization is extrapolated from the sample to the population. (Blatchford and Sumpner actually did not make such a generalization from their empirical finding.) Where this statistical generalization might become important is if, in a few years time, a replication study is made by random sampling from the similar population of the later time, so that differences between 'then and now' can be drawn.

Effective sampling of large populations is difficult and expensive. It is rare for methods of enquiry other than questionnaires to be used and in the research literature there are few educational studies that lead to statistical generalization.

So, there are unlikely to be scientific generalizations of consequence to educators, and few statistical generalizations. What hope is there for research offering predictions? Figure 1.1 on page 4 suggests that there are two major forms of outcome of empirical educational research: predictions of what may happen in particular circumstances and interpretations of what has happened in particular situations. It also suggests that there are two arenas for conducting educational research: studies of samples and studies of singularities and that, in terms of predictions the former can lead to statistical generalization and the latter to fuzzy generalization.

Fuzzy generalization is discussed in the next chapter. It is the kind of prediction, arising from empirical enquiry, that says that something *may* happen, but without any measure of its probability. It is a qualified generalization, carrying the idea of possibility but no certainty.

I was struggling to find a way of expressing this idea succinctly when I came across the paper by C. Fourali (mentioned in Chapter 1) called 'Using fuzzy logic in educational measurement' (Fourali 1997). This resolved for me a problem I have often met as an examiner of student papers. Instead of trying to give an exact mark – like 57 out of 100 for an essay, Fourali advocated giving a fuzzy mark, like 50–60 out of 100. If another examiner gave a fuzzy mark of 55–70, then it might be appropriate to combine the two and give a narrower range of 55–60 as the moderated mark. I realized that this was what I was looking for: my 'qualified' generalization could be described as a 'fuzzy' generalization.

A popular text on fuzzy logic is that of Bart Kosko – *Fuzzy Thinking* (1994). (He attributes the word 'fuzzy' to Lofti Zadeh, who began publishing on fuzzy sets in the 1960s, and chose the word in preference to 'vague'.) Kosko links the word 'fuzzy' to principles, sets, logic, systems, the past, the future, and much else! 'The fuzzy principle states that *everything is a matter of degree.*' (Kosko 1994:18.) He doesn't use the term but I can see nothing in his writing that would quarrel with the concept of fuzzy generalization.

What is a study of a singularity?

A study of a singularity is research into particular events: it includes experiment, non-random survey, and case study.

For example, consider an experiment in which one group of students is taught one way, another group taught by a different method using the same teacher, then both given the same multiple-choice test to see which group achieves better results, and then the outcome published. This is a study of a singularity: there is a boundary around the two groups of students. But it is not a case study because the analysis of the results simply concludes that one method was more successful, judged by the test, than the other. The researchers have not explored the characteristics of the teacher, or features of the teaching method, or of the students' patterns of learning. This is not to denigrate the outcome of this experiment, but to see it as simply an input–output statement without explanation.

Likewise, a questionnaire survey of, say, 10 schools to find what range of story books are used by the Key Stage 1 teachers for reading aloud to children is a study of a singularity (i.e. 10 schools at a particular time) – and not a search for statistical generalization (since not a random sample of a large population). But it is not a case study unless there is some account of why the teachers choose the books and how the children respond to them – and that is likely to entail interviews of teachers and children, and observations of children listening.

An essential feature of case study is that sufficient data are collected for researchers to be able to explore significant features of the case and to put forward interpretations for what is observed. Another essential feature is that the study is conducted mainly in its natural context. A case study of playground behaviour would require observation of playgrounds: interviews with teachers about playground behaviour would be insufficient, for it would be difficult to test for the trustworthiness of the data without triangulating them with observational data.

Case study is study of a singularity conducted in depth in natural settings.

Note

1 Did he realize that he was quoting Mr Toogood in Trollope's *Last Chronicle of Barsetshire*?

5 | How some case study research can be disseminated through fuzzy generalization and professional discourse[1]

'Do y instead of x and your pupils will learn more'

David Hargreaves's lecture to the Teacher Training Agency in 1996 was mentioned in Chapter 1 (Hargreaves 1996). He enraged many educational researchers by saying that 'the £50–£60 million we spend annually on educational research is poor value for money in terms of improving the quality of education provided in schools' (p. 1). Later in the lecture he made clear the kind of research that he was seeking, which he called 'evidence-based'. It is research which:

   (i) demonstrates conclusively that if teachers change their practice from x to y there will be a significant and enduring improvement in teaching and learning; and

  (ii) has developed an effective method of convincing teachers of the benefits of, and means to, changing from x to y.

(Hargreaves 1996: 5)

While I have a measure of agreement with Hargreaves in his criticism of much current research, I disagree with his remedy. I do not believe that there can be general statements of the kind that he seeks: teaching situations are so varied that it is rarely, if ever, possible to say with certainty 'Do y instead of x and your pupils will learn more.' These are statements in the form of scientific generalizations as discussed in Chapter 4. Teaching is such a complex activity that such simple statements just do not exist.[2]

In December 1996, the National Foundation for Educational Research held its fiftieth birthday party and Hargreaves was one of the invited speakers. He elaborated on his views as to how educational research can influence the practice of teaching and Figure 5.1 contains the diagram and part of the supporting statement which he presented (Hargreaves 1997). I

Figure 5.1 Hargreave's model of the relationship between educational research and the practice of teaching

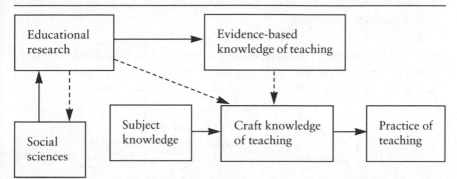

The main component of the knowledge base of teachers is the subject matter that the teacher teaches. This is mediated through craft knowledge into the practice of teaching. The craft knowledge is acquired through many processes, but there is a heavy reliance on personal experience and trial-and-error learning. The social sciences make very little impact – at least in any direct or explicit way – on craft knowledge. Educational research, itself profoundly affected by the social sciences, makes some impact on teachers' craft knowledge, but little of this is direct or explicit, and so it must be regarded as no more than a weak influence. Educational research has already generated some evidence-based knowledge which bears on craft knowledge, but it is this particular component which is most in need of strengthening if educational research is to improve the knowledge base of teachers.

argued with him at his lecture, but afterwards felt grateful for being stimulated to develop a theoretical model which I believe to be more profound and realistic. This is set out in Figure 5.2. I fear it is more complicated!

Research feeds discourse, which aids practice and policy

The model in Figure 5.2 provides answers to three questions:

- How can teachers learn from research?
- How can policy-makers learn from research?
- How can researchers learn from teachers and policy-makers?

Central to my model is the idea of *professional discourse*. I ask you to take the model bit by bit. First consider the bottom right, which indicates that what teachers do in classrooms depends upon their *craft knowledge of teaching*. This is a term that Brown and McIntyre (1993: 17) use to describe

   that part of their professional knowledge which teachers acquire primarily through their practical experience in the classroom rather than their formal training, which guides their day-to-day actions in class-rooms, which is for the most part not articulated in words, and which is brought to bear spontaneously, routinely and sometimes unconsciously on their teaching.

Figure 5.2 A model of the relationship between educational research and the practice of teaching and formation of educational policy

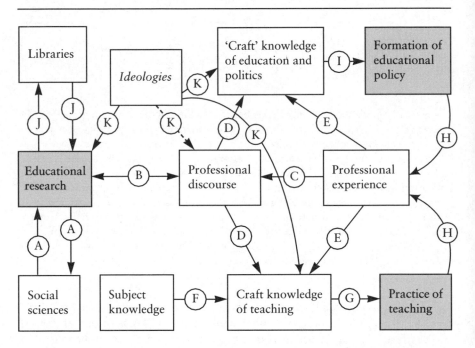

A   Educational research uses and contributes to methodologies of the other social sciences.
B   Reports of educational research contribute to professional discourse and vice versa.
C   Reports of professional experience contribute to professional discourse.
D   Professional discourse provides ideas that add to craft knowledge.
E   Professional experience provides knowledge of what has worked.
F   Subject knowledge is transmuted through craft knowledge into a teachable form.
G   Craft knowledge of teaching determines the practice of teaching.
H   Memories of practice and of policy formation are stored as professional experience.
I   'Craft' knowledge of management and politics determines policy formation.
J   Libraries store and inform educational research.
K   Usually unrecognized, ideologies impact on knowledge, discourse and research.

I am suggesting that craft knowledge of teaching is also influenced by professional discourse. This is the maelstrom of ideas, theories, facts and judgements which the individual teacher meets (through informal discussion with other teachers, reading books and articles, participating in INSET activities – and potentially on the Internet), broods on, contributes to and occasionally uses.

Turning now to the top right of the model, there is a similar juxtaposition of discourse, experience and craft knowledge involved in the formation of educational policy. Here the craft knowledge includes understanding of educational systems as well as political knowledge of how to cause change, and it is influenced by the maelstrom of ideas, theories, facts and judgements which the policy-maker meets, broods on, contributes to and occasionally uses. The policy-maker mirrors the teacher in drawing on the maelstrom.

The model recognizes that underpinning both the practice of teaching and the formation of educational policy, but often unacknowledged or even unrecognized, are a range of ideological positions. For example, policy and practice vary according to whether there is a belief that the most important role of the teacher is to transmit subject knowledge or is to foster the moral, social, creative and intellectual growth of pupils and students.

Finally, the model suggests that the role of educational research is to inform professional discourse, and to be informed by it. Research should contribute to the maelstrom of ideas, theories, facts and judgements about education. It should be something that teachers and policy-makers look for, read about, argue over, reflect on and then either reject and forget, or file away in their memory to adapt and adopt later. But here is the rub – most research writing is not memorable and much of it is not easy to get hold of.

So the question arises: how can research contribute to professional discourse in such a way that it is readily understood and remembered? In an age where we are forever battered by words, perhaps educational researchers should follow the politicians and use sound bites: those pithy phrases and sentences that convey a strong message.

Fuzzy generalizations as sound bites from research

'Do y instead of x and your pupils will learn more.' That is pithy and may be memorable. But left like that it is contrary to the truth ethic of research, for it omits the details of context and circumstance which give it meaning and it has a certainty and absoluteness which we know is never the case.

Suppose that instead the researcher said to teachers 'Do y instead of x and your pupils *may* learn more.' This is no minor change. It is not just introducing an element of uncertainty. It is not an admission of frailty in the way that the research was conducted. It is a firm reminder that there are many variables which determine whether learning takes place. And it is an invitation to teachers to enter into discourse about it: to read the evidence in support of this statement, to discuss it with anyone else who engages in x, to reflect on the issue, to test out in their own classroom the efficacy of y and to report the outcomes to whatever group will listen.

I call these general statements with built-in uncertainty 'fuzzy generalizations'.[3] With the scientific generalization there are no exceptions – and indeed in science if any are found then the statement is abandoned or revised to accommodate the new evidence. But in the use of the adjective 'fuzzy' the likelihood of there being exceptions is clearly recognized and this seems an appropriate concept for research in areas like education where human complexity is paramount.

As an example I would like to consider, and develop, the findings of one of the recent pieces of teacher research funded by the Teacher Training Agency. The teacher-researcher is Helen Morgan of Denbigh School, Milton Keynes, and her research is described in a four-page leaflet published last year by the Agency. With her permission I have condensed (and slightly rephrased) her report (Morgan 1997) as in the box on page 53.

The full report gives more details and also lists three books as 'Further reading'. These are:

Davie, R. and Galloway, D., *Listening to Children in Education,* David Fulton, 1996.
Davie, R., Upton, G. and Varma, V., *The Voice of the Child: a Handbook for Professionals,* Falmer, 1996.
Rudduck, J., Chaplain, R. and Wallace, G., *School Improvement: What Can Pupils Tell Us?,* David Fulton, 1997.

It is noteworthy that there is no account in the paper of the conceptual background to the study (as academic researchers would expect) – but the listing of these three books shows that the author is well aware of current understanding. Does the teacher reading this report need more?

The final statement is a reasonable and proper outcome of the findings within the school. What I would like to see, in a paper like this, would be a further statement in the form of a *fuzzy generalization.* This proposes that the finding may be more general and would say: 'A fuzzy generalization arising from this research is that sixth form students, through talking and answering questions about their learning experiences, may give help to their teachers towards making improvements in their teaching.' A fuzzy generalization carries an element of uncertainty. It reports that something has happened in one place and that it may also happen elsewhere. There is a possibility but no surety. There is an invitation to 'try it and see if the same happens for you'.

There is also the opportunity for the research to become cumulative. Suppose that another teacher-researcher sets out to replicate this study and finds difficulties which the first researcher had not encountered. The fuzzy generalization might be amended by adding: '. . . provided that the school has a tradition of open discussion between staff and students.' It is important to

Motivation of sixth-form students in Denbigh School in 1996

Helen Morgan

This was an enquiry into the motivation of sixth-form students in the school in which I teach: it can be described as 'large, mixed, comprehensive' and has 150 sixth-form students. The research was carried out by in-depth interviews with a small group of students and a questionnaire to year 12 students.

The findings include:

- many of the students felt that the way to make lessons enjoyable and stimulating was to have a variety of activities, including group work, debates, class discussion, role play and practical work;
- homework tasks that were interesting and relevant were most likely to motivate these students; positive feedback and high teacher expectations also motivated most students to want to complete their work;
- the main causes of these students' failure to complete homework were a lack of understanding of the task and long deadlines for its completion;
- many of the students indicated that to them the most motivating teacher styles were those that encouraged student participation, showed enthusiasm and organized individual teacher–pupil contact; and the most demotivating teacher styles were dictation, 'talking at' students and working from overhead projectors.

These findings were discussed by the staff and some changes introduced in the next year.

The overall conclusion is that these sixth-form students, through talking and answering questions about their learning experiences, gave help to their teachers towards making improvements in their teaching.

stress the relationship between a fuzzy generalization and the written report which supports it. The fuzzy generalization on its own may be memorable, but has little credence. But read in conjunction with the research report it may gain high credence and in consequence may encourage others to act on it in their own school and circumstances.

Examples of fuzzy generalizations

The Teacher Training Agency recently published a number of reports[4] from the first round of research projects commissioned as part of the Teacher

Research Grant Scheme. This scheme is part of a campaign by the Agency to get more teachers involved in doing research. Each of these reports contains four pages with a statement of aim, a 'summary of findings for this case study', an account of what was done and a contact address. From five of these I have turned a summary of the findings into fuzzy generalizations. Each contains the intellectually essential element of uncertainty and I have put the words that make that clear into italics. I hope through abbreviation I have not distorted the messages of these reports.

- Planned observation of physical education at KS2 *may* allow teachers to gain useful information about pupils' performance, give better feedback and so enhance learning. (Lucas, T. (1997) TTA Research Report.)
- In maximizing children's reading potential at KS2 and KS3 the most important factor *is likely to be* the impact of teachers' enthusiasm upon pupils' motivation and peer culture. (Hawkes, A. (1997) TTA Research Report.)
- Pupils at KS2 *may be* good predictors of their own level of mathematical understanding and there *may be* a close relationship between their confidence and their understanding. (Wilson, D. (1997) TTA Research Report.)
- In a nursery staff and parents *may* become more aware of their styles of engagement with children through watching and analysing together video clips of themselves working with children. (Whalley, M. and Arnold, C. (1997) TTA Research Report.)
- Getting secondary students to use sentence starters when writing reports on mathematical investigations *may* help and encourage them to use explanations, descriptions and reasoning and so *may* increase the quantity and quality of that writing. (Lee, C. (1997) TTA Research Report.)

Earlier I suggested that fuzzy generalizations should be the equivalent of the politician's sound bite. I guess these statements would look long-winded to a spin doctor – but they are intellectually honest. They could provide the evidence base that Hargreaves advocates. They are a succinct way in which educational research can contribute to professional discourse.

Putting research reports on the Internet

Academic researchers tend to publish their research reports in journals. Teacher researchers sometimes put their findings in journals, but at other times may print no more than a few copies which are passed around immediate colleagues. The TTA is doing an important service in funding and publishing small-scale projects by teacher researchers, but there is much more to do in making sure that teachers can access research reports. Fuzzy generalizations are of little value unless teachers can examine their justification. Many more research reports could be put on to the Internet – and when the National Grid is operational, could be accessed by teachers throughout the UK. One way of doing this is through Educatio*n-line*. This is a web service available to all educational researchers and teachers at http://www.leeds.ac.uk/educol/. It is a readily accessed compilation of research reports in what is sometimes called 'the grey literature', meaning reports which have not been published in journals. It is based at the University of Leeds and is easy to access and to contribute to.

But what is not currently available – and is needed – is a searchable index of research findings expressed as fuzzy generalizations, showing where the full research report can be found. Someone, somewhere, should fund a project to draw out fuzzy generalizations from the existing literature and make it available on the Internet to teachers everywhere. For example, there were over 500 publications on science education, over 160 on religious education, over 140 on history education and over 130 on geography education that came from higher education institutions over the four years to mid-1996 (Bassey and Constable 1997), but how does a teacher gain access to them? It isn't just a matter of locating the papers – this can often be done through the British Education Index – but of getting a very brief insight into what they contain in order to decide whether the effort of tracking the paper down is likely to be worth the trouble. This is what a searchable listing of fuzzy generalizations could offer.

Endpiece

Returning to David Hargreaves's criticisms of educational research, I believe that in large part the answer lies in how research into teaching is communicated to teachers and to policy-makers. I suggest that the idea of injecting fuzzy generalizations into professional discourse is a sensible way forward. It requires every author to end a research report with an empirical statement of what has been discovered in relation to the people studied, followed by a fuzzy generalization – or proposition[5] – which shows how the discovery *may* apply more widely. And it requires someone to index these reports and put them on the Internet for teachers and educational policy-makers to use.

Notes

1 This chapter is a slight modification of an article previously published in *Professional Development Today* (April 1998) and reproduced by kind permission of the editor.
2 In a response to my critique Hargreaves has commented, 'It depends upon what one means by "demonstrates conclusively". Bassey interprets this as meaning achieves certainty. That is one interpretation, but it is neither the only one nor the

one I intended. In education, as in medicine, most associations between x treatment and y result are likely to be a probability. Probabilities or associations can be conclusive . . . In medicine, there are treatments of first resort – the one research has shown works in many, even most, cases. But there is always the probability that, for a range of reasons, it will not work in every case . . . Educational research is usually like this. A study ends up with a general statement in the form of a probability, not a certainty.' This seems to embrace my use of the term 'fuzzy' and Hargreaves accepts that in his article (Hargreaves 1998).

3 There is an academic literature of 'fuzzy logic'. See, for example, Fourali (1997).
4 All these reports were published in 1997 by the Teacher Training Agency, London.
5 As explained in the next chapter, I am using the term 'fuzzy proposition' as a more tentative form of statement than 'fuzzy generalization'. Of course, all these statements should be seen as tentative 'approximations to the truth'.

6 | Educational case study as a prime strategy for developing educational theory which illuminates educational policy and enhances educational practice

A conceptual reconstruction of educational case study

My justification for suggesting a reconstruction of educational case study is that not only has the clarity of purpose of the case study researchers of the 1980s got lost as more and more researchers have come to perceive their small-scale studies as 'case studies', but the political world has come to recognize the potential of educational research and at the same time found its plethora of offerings often confusing and incoherent. The proposals which I am making about educational case study are set out in the box on page 58.

Inevitably there is a creative leap in putting forward a reconstruction, with some of the steps being perhaps less self-evident than others, and so I propose to take the box line-by-line and try to give a rationale for each. But first it may be helpful to the reader to recap on the previous chapters.

Chapter 1 is a personal account of concerns about some current educational research, particularly in relation to small-scale studies conceived as 'case study', and indicates the direction that the book takes. Reference is made to three major categories of case study: theory-seeking and theory-testing case studies, evaluative case studies and story-telling and picture-drawing case studies. Chapter 2 jumps straight into an example of a theory-seeking case study because this is possibly the most controversial idea. It is explored in Chapter 5, which suggests that the concept of 'fuzzy generalization', coupled with coherent case study reports, is a valuable way of bringing educational research findings into professional discourse, which in turn can influence the practice of teaching and the formation of educational policy.

An educational case study is an empirical enquiry which is:

- conducted within a localized boundary of space and time (i.e. a singularity);
- into *interesting* aspects of an educational activity, or programme, or institution, or system;
- mainly in its natural context and within an ethic of respect for persons;
- in order to inform the judgements and decisions of practitioners or policy-makers;
- or of theoreticians who are working to these ends;
- in such a way that sufficient data are collected for the researcher to be able
  - (a) to explore *significant* features of the case,
  - (b) to create *plausible* interpretations of what is found,
  - (c) to test for the trustworthiness of these interpretations,
  - (d) to construct a *worthwhile* argument or story,
  - (e) to relate the argument or story to any relevant research in the literature,
  - (f) to convey *convincingly* to an audience this argument or story,
  - (g) to provide an audit trail by which other researchers may validate or challenge the findings, or construct alternative arguments.

(Inevitably the terms 'interesting', 'significant', 'plausible', 'worthwhile' and 'convincingly' entail value judgements being made by the researcher.)

At least three types of educational case study can be conceived.

- *Theory-seeking and theory-testing case studies*: particular studies of general issues – aiming to lead to fuzzy propositions (more tentative) or fuzzy generalizations (less tentative) and conveying these, their context and the evidence leading to them to interested audiences.
- *Story-telling and picture-drawing case studies*: narrative stories and descriptive accounts of educational events, projects, programmes, institutions or systems which deserve to be told to interested audiences, after careful analysis.
- *Evaluative case studies*: enquiries into educational programmes, systems, projects or events to determine their worthwhileness, as judged by analysis by researchers, and to convey this to interested audiences.

Chapter 3 looks at some of the variety of meanings that various authors have given to 'case study' and how they have tried to tackle the problem of generalization from case study. It is from this melee of ideas that I have drawn many of the points used in my 'reconstruction'.

Chapter 4 describes the complexity of enquiry in education in general and by analysing the different forms begins to locate educational case study on the map of research in education. Chapter 7 gives some account of how case study research can be tackled.

Rationale for the elements of the reconstruction

An educational case study . . .

'Educational' locates this in the field of educational research, as opposed to discipline research in educational settings. In Chapter 4 educational research is defined as critical enquiry aimed at informing educational judgements and decisions in order to improve educational action, whereas discipline research in education is critical enquiry aimed at informing understandings of phenomena (in educational settings) which are pertinent to the discipline. Educational research is more concerned with improving action through theoretical understanding, discipline research with increasing theoretical knowledge of the discipline. The boundary is not clear-cut.

. . . an empirical enquiry

this means that it is not in the realms of reflective or creative research and that data collection is the starting point.

. . . conducted within a localized boundary of space and time

Most of the writers cited in Chapter 3 seem to agree about this. Stake attributes the concept to Louis Smith.

. . . (i.e. a singularity)

This is a term meaning that a *particular* set of events, or programme, institution, classroom etc., is the focus.

. . . into interesting aspects

Why spend time if the subject is not interesting? Kemmis (1980: 119) puts this more elegantly when he writes that the researcher 'is not an automaton shorn of human interests and programmed to execute a design devoid of socio-political consequences'.

... of an educational activity, or programme, or institution, or system

Since the defined field is educational research, i.e. about educational judgements and decisions (see Chapter 4), it is to be expected that case studies will focus on educational actions, or the consequences of educational decisions.

... mainly in its natural context and within an ethic of respect for persons

It seems unlikely that educational actions, or the consequences of educational decisions, can be studied trustworthily other than in their natural context. Four tests of 'respect for persons' are described in Chapter 7.

... in order to inform the judgements and decisions of practitioners or policy-makers

Again this is part of the definition of educational research (Chapter 4).

... or of theoreticians who are working to these ends

We should not expect that all educational research will immediately inform the concerns of practitioners or policy-makers. It is essential that researchers also build scaffolds for other researchers to climb – with the hope that ultimately the climbers will be able to inform those in the front line.

... in such a way that sufficient data are collected

Case study does require a lot of data in order that the researcher can explore features, create interpretations and test for trustworthiness (see Chapter 7). But 'sufficient' is a two-edged word meaning 'not too little, not too much'. There is no point in the case study researcher collecting more data than can be handled successfully in the time available – and that entails considerable insight and judgement.

... to explore significant *features of the case and to create* plausible *interpretations of what is found*

It is only of limited value for a researcher to conclude 'if teachers do x then y may happen'. It is much better to go beyond this and try to discover why this may happen for this may contribute to a theoretical understanding which illuminates other happenings. Kemmis's (1980: 119) enigmatic description, that 'case study consists in the imagination of the case and the invention of the study', is pertinent.

... to test for the trustworthiness of these interpretations

The critical approach should be ubiquitous in research. The question 'Does this really mean what we claim it means?' should always be in mind. Eight approaches to ensuring trustworthiness are described in Chapter 7.

... to relate the argument or story to any relevant research in the literature

If research is compared to a giant jigsaw puzzle then finding a new piece of the puzzle is of limited value unless it can be fitted into a growing area of the picture or at least stored with related pieces of the picture ready to be slotted in. The 'conceptual background' is an important section of most research papers, but the literature cited should be rigorously restricted to items that are judged strictly pertinent to the enquiry.

... to construct a worthwhile argument or story and to convey convincingly to an audience this argument or story

Unless research outcomes are expressed in a readable way for the intended audience they are likely to be ignored and the enterprise is wasted. In theory-seeking and theory-testing case studies the two-part approach hinted at in Chapter 5, in which a fuzzy generalization attracts the interest of the reader (through the abstract) and the case study report then describes the context of the finding and shows how it was arrived at, is advocated. Such case studies tend to be shorter than the evaluation and story-telling kinds. The latter sometimes need considerable detail in order to demonstrate that the story is significant. Thus the case study in Chapter 9 – on classroom organization patterns in primary schools in the 1980s – gives extensive detail of how three teachers organized their classrooms. This gives credence to the claim, at the end of the case report, that: 'before the Education Reform Act of 1988 and the continuing interference of the state in classrooms, there were dedicated competent teachers fully committed to the needs of the children in their care who were quite able to work effectively without official monitoring and state harassment.'

... to provide an audit trail by which other researchers may validate or challenge the findings, or construct alternative arguments

This idea is developed in Chapter 7. It endeavours to give access to others of the evidence which points to the trustworthiness of the study but also enables them to exercise their own creativity in finding alternative interpretations. An important aspect of this proposed in Chapter 7 is that as standard practice researchers should invite a colleague to conduct an audit of their research and issue a simple certificate on the trustworthiness of the study.

The categorization of case study in this reconstruction

Theory-seeking and theory-testing case studies

These are particular studies of general issues. The singularity is chosen because it is expected in some way to be typical of something more general. The focus is the issue rather than the case as such. It is what Stake (1995) calls 'instrumental case study'. If I have understood him correctly, my 'theory-seeking' case study is what Yin (1993) calls 'exploratory' and my 'theory-testing' case study is what he calls 'explanatory'. Adelman *et al.* (1980) saw it as 'a bounded system (the case) selected as an instance of a class' (see Chapter 3). I have chosen my form of words because it makes perfectly clear what the theoretical intention of such case studies is, and how one leads to the other. Introducing the concepts of 'fuzzy propositions' (more tentative) and 'fuzzy generalizations' (less tentative), as discussed in Chapter 5 in relation to professional discourse and the development of educational practice and policy, is an attempt to find an effective way of communicating research findings to those who may use them. Holligan's case study in Chapter 2 is an example of a theory-seeking case study and Chapter 9 contains theory-seeking case studies embedded in a story-telling case study.

Story-telling and picture-drawing case studies

These are what Stake (1995) calls 'intrinsic case study', Yin (1993) calls 'descriptive case study' and Adelman *et al.* (1980) saw as a given 'bounded system' within which issues are studied. But these include evaluation studies and I believe it is better to recognize the differences rather than merge them all together.

Story-telling and picture-drawing case studies are both analytical accounts of educational events, projects, programmes or systems aimed at illuminating theory. Story-telling is predominantly a narrative account of the exploration and analysis of the case, with a strong sense of a time line. Picture-drawing is predominantly a descriptive account, drawing together the results of the exploration and analysis of the case. Both should give theoretical insights, expressed as a claim to knowledge, but this is more discursive than the fuzzy propositions and generalizations of theory-seeking and theory-testing case study.

'Picture-drawing' seems to me to be a neat parallel to the term 'story-telling', but to some it may seem too primary school oriented. They may prefer to call it 'portrayal'. Crossley and Vulliamy (1984) have drawn attention to the value of this kind of case study for research into comparative education:

> the potential of such work within the field is considerable. Case-study need not be purely descriptive; it need not be limited to the micro-level; and it need not ignore comparative analysis itself. By focusing upon the complexities of educational *practice*, it can lead to important modifications of both educational policies and comparative theories of educational systems.
>
> (Crossley and Vulliamy 1984: 204)

These same authors have since brought together a great deal of evidence supporting this contention, in their editorship of *Qualitative Research in Developing Countries* (Crossley and Vulliamy 1997).

Chapter 8 is an example of a story-telling case study (containing the report of an evaluation) and Chapter 9 (as noted above) is a story-telling case study with other cases embedded in it. Chapter 10 is a picture-drawing case study giving the results of a detailed study of the experience of student-teachers on final teaching practice.

Evaluative case studies

These are enquiries which set out to explore some educational programme, system, project or event in order to focus on its worthwhileness. The case may be tightly structured as an examination of the extent to which the programme's stated objectives have been achieved, or it may be illuminative in the phrase coined by Parlett and Hamilton (1977), as described in Chapter 3. It may be formative (in helping the development of the programme) or summative (in assessing it after the event). It draws on theoretical notions but is not necessarily intended to contribute to the development of theory – and in that sense is different from the other kinds of educational case study described above.

Chapter 8 is an example of evaluative case study work, which, to give coherence within this book, I have embedded in a story-telling report.

Comment

Following Stenhouse (1988: 49), I have omitted ethnographic case study from this list, seeing it as relating to the disciplines of anthropology and sociology rather than education. There is no mention of case study in action research, because although case study may be a stage in an action research programme, I take this to be covered by the discussion of evaluative case study – and the overall account to be covered by the discussion of story-telling case study.

Categorization is a dangerous game and I hope the reader will recognize this. Some educational case studies, as defined in the reconstruction, will not fit the categorization because they either overlap too many categories or seem to stand outside them. The justification of trying to categorize is in the hope that it will be useful more times than not. And it does serve to point to the importance of educational theory in different forms.

7 | Methods of enquiry and the conduct of case study research

Introduction

Case study research, as described in Chapter 6, needs to be conducted in such a way that sufficient data are collected for the researcher to be able:

(a) to explore *significant* features of the case;
(b) to create *plausible* interpretations of what is found;
(c) to test for the trustworthiness of these interpretations;
(d) to construct a *worthwhile* argument or story;
(e) to relate the argument or story to any relevant research in the literature;
(f) to convey *convincingly* to an audience this argument or story;
(g) to provide an audit trail by which other researchers may validate or challenge the findings, or construct alternative arguments.

This chapter suggests some of the ways in which these may be achieved. It starts with suggesting one way of dividing the enquiry into stages, and gives an illustration of what these stages may mean. This leads to a discussion of research ethics, which in turn opens up the issue of trustworthiness (arising from the ethic of respect for truth) and ethical guidelines (arising from the ethic of respect for persons). This provides a starting point for discussion of data collecting methods, data analysis and different styles of writing.

Stages in conducting case study research

In order to write about methods of enquiry and the conduct of case study research, it simplifies matters to divide the process into a number of stages. But the reader must recognize that the procedures described here will only rarely be in accord with the processes of actual studies. Research is a creative activity and every enquiry has its own unique character; it is also a systematic activity and so the idea that it goes through stages, whether or not the ones described here, is important; and it is a critical activity and so there need to be procedures stage by stage for ensuring that the findings are trustworthy. The following account of stages of research is summarized in the following list and illustrated by a hypothetical example of a researcher who monitors the experience of a school as it goes through an inspection.

Stage 1: identifying the research as an issue, problem or hypothesis.
Stage 2: asking research questions and drawing up ethical guidelines.
Stage 3: collecting and storing data.
Stage 4: generating and testing analytical statements.
Stage 5: interpreting or explaining the analytical statements.
Stage 6: deciding on the outcome and writing the case report.
Stage 7: finishing and publishing.

Stage 1: Identifying the research as an issue, problem or hypothesis

Going back to first principles, research is about trying to make a claim to knowledge, or wisdom, on the basis of systematic, creative and critical enquiry. It is about trying to discover something that was not known before and then communicating that finding to others. A helpful way of thinking about that 'something' is to see it as an *issue* to be explored, or a *problem* to be tackled, or a *hypothesis* to be tested. Deciding initially on one of these provides a platform for asking research questions.

It is not a rigid classification of mutually exclusive possibilities. Often a research intention can be expressed under more than one of these headings by juggling the words describing it, but nevertheless one of the three may be judged to be the most suitable way of describing the research at a particular stage of enquiry. Later this may change and another of the three might be the more apt way of seeing it.

A *research hypothesis* is a tentative statement or conjecture that is in a form which can be tested. For example:

> That the introduction of the Literacy Hour in this school will within
> two years have raised the percentage of children achieving level 2 in
> English at KS1.

It enables clear research questions to be asked which should provide evidence which either supports the hypothesis or refutes it. The research purpose is to test the hypothesis.

A *research problem* identifies a difficulty which often can be expressed as a contradiction between what is happening and what someone would like to happen. For example:

> The introduction of the Literacy Hour in this school requires children
> to be in year groups and since classes are currently organised with two
> year groups in each class there are going to be problems in ensuring
> that the rest of the curriculum is covered effectively.

The popular idea that where there is a problem the job of the researcher is to find a solution is usually unrealistic. The research purpose is more likely to be to formulate and try out ways in which the problem may be better understood and so be alleviated or the difficulty reduced, and to this end appropriate research questions need to be asked.

A *research issue* is the least defined category of research. It describes an area for enquiry where no problems or hypotheses have yet been clearly expressed that will direct the enquiry. For example:

How will the introduction of the Literacy Hour affect our school?

The research purpose here is to strive to focus the issue through asking pertinent research questions.

Early on in a research programme the question should be asked: what kind of report is it envisaged will eventually be written? Will it be a story-telling, or an evaluative, or a theory-seeking/theory-testing case study? The last of these obviously links with the idea of a hypothesis, while story-telling and evaluation tend to be linked to either issues or problems.

> Suppose that at the start the investigation is identified as a research issue with the over-arching question, 'What is the experience of this particular school during an Ofsted inspection at this particular time?' This is the question that defines the claim to knowledge that it is intended to make when the research is done, but it is not a research question in a technical sense because it does not set the agenda for data collection and analysis. Suppose that the end point of the research is intended to be a story-telling case study.

Stage 2: Asking research questions and drawing up ethical guidelines

A research question is the engine which drives the train of enquiry. It should be formulated in such a way that it sets the immediate agenda for research, enables data to be collected and permits analysis to get started; it should also establish the boundaries of space and time within which it will operate. If this 'engine' is found to be under-powered, or breaks down, or is pulling the train in the wrong direction, it should be replaced – pronto! It should be expected that research questions will be modified or replaced as the enquiry develops – but without them the journey will be slow and chaotic.

> Suppose these research questions set the agenda for action by our researcher:
>
> • What is the official purpose of an Ofsted inspection? (Study official documents.)
> • What procedures are involved in an Ofsted inspection? (Study official documents.)

- What are the contacts between the Ofsted inspection team and the school, before, during and after the inspection? (Study school correspondence, ask questions of head.)
- What are the expectations and views of the headteacher and classroom teachers about five weeks before the inspection? (Conduct recorded interviews.)
- How did the chair of governors (who is a parent) view the parents' meeting with the inspectors? (Have conversation and make notes afterwards.)
- What are the expectations and views of the headteacher and classroom teachers about five days before the inspection? (Conduct brief interviews, with notes written during discussion.)
- What events during the inspection week surfaced in staffroom discussions? (Observe and participate in conversations in staff room before school, during breaks and lunch times, and after school – notes written as a four-day journal by the researcher.)
- What was the headteacher's account of the inspection day-by-day? (Record brief interviews at around 10 a.m. each day.)
- What was said at the oral report stage at the end of the week? (Record head's account in interview.)
- What were the views of the headteacher and classroom teachers during the week following the inspection? (Conduct recorded interviews.)
- What issues are raised by the formal report? (Read the inspection report.)
- What are the views of headteacher and classroom teachers on the issues raised by the inspectors? (Conduct brief recorded interviews.)
- What are the views of the chair of governors on the inspector's report? (Have conversation and make notes afterwards.)

Each of these questions identifies actions to be taken by the researcher and when each should happen. This is the essence of research questions: that they define what the researcher should do. They also point to various ethical features of the study.

It is important to note that this array of data, complex as it may seem, will only scratch the surface of the school's experience. Another researcher, working in the same situation, might have chosen to interview the inspectors, or the parents, or the children, or have negotiated the opportunity to observe the inspectors in the classrooms.

Parallel to devising research questions should be the drawing up of ethical guidelines for the project. This is discussed later in this chapter. Perhaps the researcher and head will agree the following guidelines:

1 The transcripts or reports of every interview will be shown to the
   interviewee as soon as possible after the event and will only be
   included in the case record in a form agreed by the interviewee, and
   with a pseudonym. Inclusion in the case record will mean that the
   researcher may cite the evidence in the case report.
2 The case report will require the agreement of the head before it is
   made public, and the head reserves the right to request that the
   school be given a pseudonym with its location disguised.

Stage 3: Collecting and storing data

Case study research has no specific methods of data collection or of analysis which are unique to it as a method of enquiry. It is eclectic and in preparing a case study researchers use whatever methods seem to them to be
appropriate and practical. One study may predominantly use questionnaires, another interviews, another observations and another documents –
and within each of these descriptions there are endless variations. I urge
researchers to be creative and adventurous in their choice of data collection
methods. In doing so they should be governed not by traditional views of
data collection but by considerations of research ethics.

Later, some of these data-collecting methods are discussed in some detail,
but here it is worth making two points which, although superficially obvious, are ones that from time to time we all fall down on. First, be systematic
in recording data: for example, noting date and time and place, and keeping
back-up files. Second, don't collect more data than you have the time and
energy to analyse. With this in mind, it is worthwhile beginning to analyse
data as they come in, rather than waiting until all data are collected.

> Painstakingly our researcher collects the data. Some of the research
> questions may not be answered in the way expected, sometimes it may
> not be possible to meet the people whom it was planned to meet and
> at other times different sources of data will be manifest and perhaps
> captured by the researcher. No doubt from time to time she wishes
> that fewer research questions had been posed!
>
> Eventually it is all put together systematically in a series of files on
> the researcher's computer – one file for each of the research questions,
> and one for the incidental items of data which hadn't been planned
> for. This forms the start of the *case record* of the research. Where
> there are ethical issues about the ownership of data there is a rigorous
> system for knowing when something has been cleared for use in the
> final report. (For example, interview transcripts may be put into a
> different font from the rest of the data until they have been cleared.)
>
> As the researcher puts the raw data on to the computer – or edits
> what an assistant has typed in – ideas begin to formulate in her mind

of possible modes of analysis, or of the trustworthiness of the data, or of other issues which should be explored. These are inserted into the data files as *annotations* – perhaps in a different size or font or in italics – marked with the date on which they are entered.

To facilitate the sorting process (see below) it is advisable to section the raw data into *data items* (for example, a question and answer from an interview transcript might be one data item) and label each so that later, when a copy has been sorted, items can still be tracked back to source.

In addition the computer has the day-by-day journal of the researcher – with entries showing who was seen, when, where and why; and speculative notes of ideas about the research which disturbed her sleep etc., but which can't be annotated to particular parts of the raw data.

Stage 4: Generating and testing analytical statements

Case study work usually produces a great deal of raw data, and a useful way of handling and trying to make sense of the data is analysis which seeks to condense them into meaningful statements. These analytical statements need to be firmly based on the raw data, and may suggest the need for more specific data to be collected.

As a first stage, analytical statements need to be generated which give concise answers to the research questions. Thus the research question, 'What is the official purpose of an Ofsted inspection?', presumably can be simply answered by a quote from an official document. But the research question, 'What are the expectations and views of the headteacher and classroom teachers about five days before the inspection?', will require careful reading and re-reading of the interview notes, the formulation of draft analytical statements (i.e. hypotheses) and the careful testing of these statements (and amendment where necessary) against the data. The outcome should be analytical statements which are in accord with the data. If the data items and analytical statements are systematically coded (e.g. DI1, DI2 . . . and AS1, AS2 . . .) then cross-referencing can be inserted.

Having done this, the researcher may try to generate some second-level analytical statements that illuminate the original issue by seeking to portray accurately the experience of the school during the inspection. They will arise from reading and reflecting on the first round of analytical statements, and going back to the raw data: they may be stimulated by the annotations that have been made to the raw data. The analysis could be based on a time frame, i.e. how people perceived it before, during and after the inspection. Or it could focus on the different participants and show, for example, how the governors perceived it differently from the staff. Or it might take issues like power, professionalism or teacher stress, and build analytical statements around these. (Clearly it is easier to relate the data to ideas such as these if they were in the researcher's mind from the outset of data collection – but they may be ideas that have only surfaced during the enquiry.) This part of the research is very creative and, of course, other researchers using the same data might come up with different constructs for basing the analysis on.

For example, this analytical statement might be generated:

AS100 Throughout the period, from the announcement that inspection would take place until well after the report was received, and particularly during the period of classroom visits, all the teaching staff, without exception, showed signs of high level stress.

Analytical statements always need to be tested against the data. They are, of course, initially in the form of tentative hypotheses. It is here that computer search facilities are helpful. If each of the analytical statements is given a code (in this example AS100) and this code is inserted in the case record against data items or earlier analytical statements which seem relevant to the proposed new statement, it becomes a relatively simple operation to make a copy of all the files and then sort them according to the coding.

The likely result of a first testing of the analytical statements is that some stand, some need modifying and others lack verity and are rejected. Analysis and data testing is an iterative process which continues until the researcher feels confident that the analytical statements are trustworthy.

Stage 5: Interpreting or explaining the analytical statements

This is where 'how?' and 'why?' questions are brought to bear on the analytical statements in an attempt to provide understanding of the way things are. Interpretations are associated with particular individuals or groups of people, while explanations tend to be attempts at expressing cause-and-effect relationships.

Consider the above example (AS100) of an analytical statement. If the researcher simply reports this as the conclusion to the research it will be of little interest and people will say, 'Fancy putting all that effort in and telling us what we already knew.' But suppose that she explores the data further to seek an interpretation of why this was the case.

She might put forward a number of alternative hypotheses to explain this stress, such as:

AS100/E1 that they feared for their job security;

AS100/E2 that they were worried sick at the idea of an inspector in the classroom and the children being difficult;

AS100/E3 that being given a judgement in a brown envelope on their professional calibre was a nightmare;

AS100/E4 that they were concerned that the school be judged to be failing and about the subsequent actions of parents.

Our researcher now searches the data items already tagged as supporting AS100 for evidence that supports these alternative explanations as particularly important in this school at this time. Additionally, she might conduct some follow-up interviews in order to collect more raw data that might support or refute these explanatory hypotheses. (Note that at this stage the enquiry has refocused from being about an issue to being a testing of hypotheses.) Eventually, let us suppose, her *interpretation* of the evidence is that E4 was unimportant and that the major cause of the stress identified in AS100 was explanation E2, with E1 and E3 also contributing to a less extent.

Yet another line of developing the research might be to refocus the enquiry as a problem expressed like this:

High level stress is undesirable; how could the inspection have been organized to reduce this stress?

Searching the data with this question in mind might reveal some pointers; follow up interviews might also be important.

Stage 6: Deciding on the outcome and writing the case report

Here what happens depends upon the type of case study being prepared. A theory-seeking/theory-testing case study will give an empirical statement of findings, supported by sufficient evidence to give the reader confidence, and perhaps leading to a fuzzy proposition (more tentative) or a fuzzy generalization (less tentative) of what may be the case elsewhere. An evaluative case study will respond to the original brief, again supported by sufficient evidence to give the reader confidence. A story-telling case study will tell the story in whatever way the researcher judges to be appropriate for the chosen audience, but as with the other types, drawing carefully on the evidence to convince the reader of the story's trustworthiness.

Our example might be reported in several different ways. It could be reported as a theory-seeking study with an empirical conclusion that:

the Ofsted inspection caused high levels of stress in this school for the following reasons . . .

This might lead to a fuzzy generalization that:

Ofsted inspections may cause high levels of stress in any school for the following reasons . . .

It could be reported as an evaluation, which might develop along this line:

the Ofsted inspection caused high levels of stress in this school and some serious consequences for the school were these . . .

It could be reported as a story which portrays the experience of this school during the Ofsted inspection and tries through careful use of narrative and description to convey the stress felt by the staff in a way that might cause policy-makers to reconsider what Ofsted inspections achieve.

In reporting on a theory-seeking/theory-testing case study it is expected that the researcher will refer to related research as reported in the literature and show how this study fits into the general picture. This is often referred to as the 'conceptual background' to the study.

Stage 7: Finishing and publishing

Before you accept the euphoria of having finished a study it is suggested that a colleague should be invited to conduct an audit – as described at the end of this chapter.

Then take heed of Michael Faraday's maxim: work, finish, publish. Later in this chapter there is a section on 'Writing case reports', but here it is worth reflecting on what 'publishing' means. In terms of research it means communicating a claim to knowledge to an audience in writing. It may be perhaps 50 copies of a handful of A4 sheets stapled together and distributed to interested people. Or it may be such a report put on to the Internet – for example, through Education-line, which electronically publishes reports like this – sometimes termed the 'grey literature'. It may be a paper published in a professional or academic journal, or a four-sided pamphlet distributed by some agency to schools, or an article in The Times Educational Supplement. But it may be a presentation at a conference, or conceivably an account recorded on video or audio tape. Often it will be several of these forms – each aimed at promoting the kind of professional discourse described in Chapter 5.

The ethics of research

It is helpful to discuss research ethics under three headings: respect for democracy, respect for truth and respect for persons.

- *Respect for democracy*. Researchers in a democratic society can expect certain freedoms: the freedom to investigate and to ask questions; the freedom to give and to receive information; the freedom to express ideas and to criticize the ideas of others; and the freedom to publish research findings. These freedoms are essentially subject to responsibilities imposed by the ethics of respect for truth and respect for persons: provided that these responsibilities are honoured, researchers can expect the freedom to do these things without endangering themselves or their livelihood.[1]
- *Respect for truth*. Researchers are expected to be truthful in data collection, analysis and the reporting of findings. This means that they should not deceive others intentionally. Equally, it means that they should try not to deceive themselves and others unintentionally. It is here that trustworthiness becomes significant, as described below.
- *Respect for persons*. Researchers, in taking data from persons, should do so in ways which recognize those persons' initial ownership of the data and which respect them as fellow human beings who are entitled to dignity and privacy.

The problem with these ethical values is that they can clash. In trying to tell the story, the researcher may claim the democratic right to investigate and to publish the findings, and may insist that the evidence is trustworthy and portrays the truth of what happened, but may find that the people who provided the evidence insist on the privacy to which they are entitled. In the Nottinghamshire Staff Development Project Evaluation reported in Chapter 8 I identified an important issue in one school in the course of interviews with staff, but could not persuade the head to let me publish the relevant data in my report. I dropped the issue.

By contrast, most journalists do not concern themselves about the ethic of respect for persons, and in demanding the right to investigate and to publish what they perceive as the truth (which may be challenged in the libel courts) claim that their work is of public interest and so publication is essential. One consequence is that teachers, for example, are wary of talking to journalists, but generally sympathetic to researchers. The British Educational Research Association Ethical Guidelines seek to strengthen the bond between researcher and researched by adding to the above three ethical values a fourth: respect for educational research itself. This enjoins researchers not to conduct their research in ways which will damage the future enquiries of other researchers, but to seek to enhance the image of research.

Trustworthiness in case study research

The concepts of reliability and validity are vital concepts in surveys and experiments – but not in case study research. In the simplest analysis reliability is the extent to which a research fact or finding can be repeated, given the same circumstances, and validity is the extent to which a research fact or finding is what it is claimed to be. Validity can be analysed in a number of ways.[2] For example, internal validity is concerned with the relationships between cause and effect, and external validity is concerned with the extent to which a cause-and-effect relationship can be generalized to other contexts. In case study research these concepts are problematic.

A case study is the study of a singularity which is chosen because of its interest to the researcher (or the researcher's sponsor) and, it is hoped, the reader of the case report. It is not chosen as a 'typical' example in the sense that typicality is empirically demonstrated, and so issues of external validity are not meaningful. If it is a theory-seeking case study there may be a fuzzy cause-and-effect relationship where internal validity can be examined, but evaluation case studies and story-telling case studies do not necessarily involve cause and effect.

As an alternative to reliability and validity, Lincoln and Guba put forward the concept of *trustworthiness* in 1985 in *Naturalistic Inquiry*,[3] and in my view this successfully illuminates the ethic of respect for truth in case study research. The following draws on their account (Lincoln and Guba 1985: Chapter 11) but simplifies it, introduces some additional concepts and is expressed in a developmental sequence of the last four stages of a research project as described earlier. The summary[4] below is followed by discussion of each of the eight questions.

At the third stage: collection of raw data

1　Has there been prolonged engagement with data sources?
2　Has there been persistent observation of emerging issues?
3　Have raw data been adequately checked with their sources?

At the fourth stage: analysis of raw data

4　Has there been sufficient triangulation of raw data leading to analytical statements?

At the fifth stage: interpretation of analytical statements

5　Has the working hypothesis, or evaluation, or emerging story been systematically tested against the analytical statements?
6　Has a critical friend thoroughly tried to challenge the findings?

At the sixth and seventh stages: reporting of the research

7　Is the account of the research sufficiently detailed to give the reader confidence in the findings?
8　Does the case record provide an adequate audit trail?

---

1 *Has there been prolonged engagement with data sources?* 'Prolonged engagement' is a concept introduced by Lincoln and Guba (1985). It is about spending enough time on a case in order to be immersed in its issues, build the trust of those who provide data and try to avoid misleading ideas.

2 *Has there been persistent observation of emerging issues?* 'Persistent observation' is another phrase from Lincoln and Guba (1985). This is about thorough searching for tentative salient features of the case and then focusing attention on them – either to discover that they are not relevant or to try to gain some clear understanding of them.

3 *Have raw data been adequately checked with their sources?* It is good practice after an interview to take the report of the interview back to the interviewee to check that it is an accurate record and that the interviewee is willing for it to be used in the research. Sometimes people realize that they have not said what they meant to say and this provides an opportunity to put the record straight. Recorded observations (for example, of teachers' actions in classrooms) can sometimes likewise be offered for comment.

4 *Has there been sufficient triangulation of raw data leading to analytical statements?* This question presupposes that the researcher, in searching for significant features of the case, brings together data from different sources, or from the same source but by different methods of enquiry, or by using different observers, and makes analytical statements which credibly illuminate these features. Triangulation is a term taken from surveying, where it is a means of accurately pinpointing a place. In social science research it means trying to strengthen confidence in a statement.

5 *Has the working hypothesis, evaluation or emerging story been systematically tested against the analytical statements?* There is often a creative leap in research which is difficult to explain in terms of how it happened. That doesn't matter – what does matter is that the end point of this leap – be it a hypothesis, or an evaluative statement, or an emerging storyline – is carefully and systematically tested against the analytical statements which have been made about the raw data.

6 *Has a critical friend thoroughly tried to challenge the findings?* Lincoln and Guba (1985) called this 'peer debriefing', but the action research movement has brought the idea of a critical friend into prominence. This is someone who plays devil's advocate in questioning the research processes and outcomes. It requires a friend giving the researcher some of that precious commodity, time. And it requires openness and humility in order to ensure that the friendship survives. It is invaluable in strengthening a research project.

7 *Is the account of the research sufficiently detailed to give the reader confidence in the findings?* The writing of a case study report needs to strike the right balance between saying too much (by either confusing the readers or, worse, wearing them out so that they fail to finish reading) and saying too little (and not giving the readers sufficient evidence for them to feel that the conclusions are valid). But if the case study is to be of value it must convey a justification for its end point.

8 *Does the case record provide an adequate audit trail?* The concept of an audit trail again is something that Lincoln and Guba (1985) have written about, although they give the credit to an unpublished doctoral dissertation by Halpern (1983). It is the idea that the researcher should keep systematically a record which would allow an auditor to check stage-by-stage on the research in order to certify that the conclusions are justified. However, it was Stenhouse who gave credence to the term 'case record' in the early 1980s (Stenhouse 1988: 52) as the 'substantial collection of documents, observer's notes, interview transcripts, statistics, and the like' which form the basis from which the case report is written. A well ordered case record is evidence that the research was carried out systematically and could be the basis for an effective audit.

Respect for persons in case study research

Case study involves taking extensive data from the people being questioned or observed, trying to extract some meaning that was not apparent or was not substantiated before, and then trying to express this in a cogent form to an audience. In order to sustain the concept of 'respect for persons' and, indeed, in order to obtain their cooperation in providing data, it is usual to negotiate the extent to which data taken from them can be used in writing the report. The box below suggests four questions which are usually important and the answers to which could form what are often called the 'ethical guidelines' for a research project. This simply means a statement of the agreed principles which will govern the conduct of the enquiry. Each question is discussed in turn.

At the first stage

1 Has permission been given to conduct the research in terms of the stage one identification of an issue, problem, or hypothesis, in this particular setting?

At the third stage

2 What arrangements have been agreed for transferring the ownership of the record of utterances and actions to the researcher, thus enabling the latter to use these in compiling the case record?

At the sixth stage

3 What arrangements have been agreed for either identifying or concealing the contributing individuals and the particular setting of the research in the case report?

4 What arrangements have been agreed for giving permission to publish the case report?

Has permission been given to conduct the research?

In Hong Kong a research student once told me that his proposed research would entail interviewing teachers in a morning school and an afternoon school (same site, different principals, teachers and students) in order to test the hypothesis that the rapid turnover of staff in the morning school was because the principal of this school was a less effective communicator and manager than the principal of the afternoon school. His plans crumbled when I asked whether he had sought permission from the two principals to conduct this research in their schools.

Most researchers find that a simple letter from someone in authority is sufficient. Discussion of the issues raised in the remaining questions may best be left until later, when the research has been planned in more detail.

What arrangements have been agreed for transferring ownership of the record?

The usual research convention is that utterances and actions of fellow professionals (teachers etc.), as recorded on tape and then transcribed, or as recorded directly into the researcher's notebook, should not be entered into the case record of the research until the person concerned has had an opportunity to read the draft version, amend it if she or he considers it does not represent the truth and agree that it may be put in the case record.

Similar practice is usual with other adults, but the researcher needs to judge whether it is appropriate in the circumstances of the enquiry. For example, this quite sophisticated procedure may frighten off some people, and anyone with poor reading skills would find it very daunting.

This validating-the-evidence procedure is not usually done with children, although often their parents are asked for permission for them to be interviewed. Most researchers will say to children, 'May I ask you some questions?' and respect any rejection. Where circumstances preclude such practice it is appropriate to explain this in the case report.

What arrangements have been agreed for either identifying or concealing individuals and settings?

Agreement should be reached, preferably before the research data collection starts, as to whether the people will be named, given a pseudonym or remain anonymous, and likewise whether the setting (for example, the school) will be named or given a pseudonym or remain anonymous. Disguising people or places is not easy, and certainly it needs to be remembered that people working within an institution are likely to recognize their colleagues in a 'disguised' report, particularly those with senior responsibilities. Anonymity is not necessarily the best approach.

What arrangements have been agreed for giving permission to publish the case report?

Having invested a great deal of personal effort in the case study the researcher will want to see it published and in terms of the ethic of respect for democracy will see it as essential. But what if, for example, the head-teacher of the school in which the study was conducted is unhappy and considers that the report portrays the teachers in the school as ineffective – while agreeing that this is true? This is one reason why it is important to clarify the guidelines for publication before starting the research.

Ethical guidelines and ethical dilemmas

Drawing up a set of ethical guidelines which respond to the above questions is likely to be helpful, but does not necessarily resolve all problems. Stenhouse (1985: 53) raised an important issue when he wrote: 'In educational case study where the purpose of the research is to improve educational practice and hence the lot of children and the professionalism of teachers there is at least some room for a consideration of the responsibility of subjects to take risks on professional grounds.' What should a researcher do if permission for conducting a piece of research is refused by those in authority? What should a researcher do in a situation where the likelihood of being given permission is very low and the researcher considers that it is better not to ask and so avoid the risk of the charge of disobedience? Would my Hong Kong student have been justified in conducting his enquiry into the relative competence of two principals on the grounds that it could have led to a marked improvement in the educational provision of one of the schools?

It is usual to reject the idea of covert research, but it may be that because of this view important research into some issues of policy and of practice is not conducted. There may be justification for researchers taking risks. Certainly there are no easy answers to this issue.

What can be said, however, is that where there is tension between respect for democracy, for truth and for persons, at least the researcher should take careful counsel from fellow researchers, and in the case report there should be thorough discussion of the issues involved and how and why the researcher has chosen to resolve them.

Archive, case record and case report

When a case study is completed there may be a number of sets of documents containing different aspects of the enquiry. One way of organizing these is to distinguish between archive, case record and case report.

The *archive* is the complete set of documents involved in the enquiry. It includes the rough notes and jottings made during interviews, the draft transcripts or reports of interviews, possibly the tapes themselves and the agreed versions of transcripts. It contains observation records, and any diaries that may have been kept by researcher or participants. It has photocopies or notes of articles which have contributed to the account of the conceptual background. Analytical statements, in both draft and final form, are there and writings striving to interpret the findings. It also has the final version of both the case record and the case report. All of these are contained in a filing cabinet, or tea chest, or set of cardboard boxes, and stored in some systematic way that would enable statements in the case report to be tracked back to the original data. Perhaps it rarely happens to this level of perfection, but the idea of a thorough archive is commendable. It needs to be seen as a secure depository, for some of the raw data may not have been approved by those who provided them and where names have been anonymized these changes need to be respected. It is not unreasonable to put a destruction date on such an archive, usually on grounds of lack of long-term storage.

The *case record* is the agreed interview transcripts and observation reports, the final versions of analytical statements, the interpretive writings, the final draft of conceptual background statements, the day-by-day journal of the research, and other documents. It is a subset of the archive. These are the papers which eventually are approved for public access and polished in their format, but which are likely to be too voluminous to hold the attention of anyone but the most dedicated reader. They are the researcher's source for writing the case report. It is likely that all of the case record will be in the form of a set of files on the researcher's computer – with suitable back-up copies in case of computer failure!

The *case report* is often called the 'case study', although in reality it is just the end point and the complete enquiry is the case study. The case report is constructed from the case record to serve the end of theory-seeking, theory-testing, evaluation, an educational story or an educational portrayal. Whereas the case record has been compiled as the working document of the researcher exploring an issue, or working at a problem, or testing a hypothesis, the case report needs to be written with an audience in mind. Indeed, it can be possible to write several different case reports from the same case record – with different audiences in mind, or focusing on different aspects of the study.

These descriptions are not watertight. The transitions from archive to case record, and from case record to case report, are not clear-cut. Are the processes of annotation and coding of data items against analytical statements, as mentioned earlier, something that happens to the archived documents or to documents within the case record? Of course, it doesn't really matter. What is important is that the process is conducted in a sufficiently systematic way to ensure that the researcher can work effectively within the ethic of trustworthiness and the ethic of respect for persons. The idea of archive, case record and case report may give this systematic approach.

Data collection methods

There are three major methods of collecting research data: asking questions (and listening intently to the answers), observing events (and noting carefully what happens) and reading documents.

A number of substantial texts exist which give detailed instructions for designing questionnaires, conducting various types of interviews and making observational studies. Much is usually made of the extent to which the data collection is tightly structured prior to the event, or is open-ended so that the researcher can 'think on her feet' and adapt the questions or observations to the situation as it develops. These texts can be unhelpful to the new researcher engaging in a case study because they can be taken to imply that strict rules exist for data collection. My advice to the researcher is this, 'Work out your own methods – from a clear ethical standpoint, and based on your research questions.' This is why this chapter contains a discussion of research ethics, including tests for trustworthiness and tests for respect for persons. But having said this, the reader may think me remiss if there is not some account of data collection methods here.

Asking questions; and listening intently to the answers

Interviews inevitably have a sense of formality. The researcher has asked the respondent if he will give some time and reveal some of his thinking, not in an idle chat but in a situation where the researcher will record it, or write it down. The respondent may be pleased to contribute, or frightened, or irritated because of the time taken. He may not have previously given deep thought to the issue and may actually be constructing his position during the interview. His answers are likely to be influenced by his view of the researcher, and by his concerns of who will see her report. The social skills of the interviewer in relating sensitively to the respondent and her cognitive skills in discovering what he thinks are all important.

Most researchers like to interview with a tape recorder and today most teachers and nearly all children can cope with this, but some lay people (for example, some governors and parents) may prefer the researcher to make notes rather than a recording. The advantage of recording for the researcher is that she can attend to the direction rather than the detail of the interview and then listen intently afterwards.

There are two major approaches to handling tapes. One is to transcribe everything that is on the tape. This takes between five and ten times as long to produce as the actual interview, and usually contains a large amount of redundant text because of the way that most of us in speech repeat ourselves, get side-tracked and 'delete' sentences by leaving them unfinished. The alternative is to paraphrase and make a shortened report of the tape. With experience this can be done in about twice the time of the interview. In choosing this method the researcher must recognize that some of the nuances of the tape will be lost: if one view of data analysis is that it is the process of reducing data to manageable proportions, this is its beginning.

The transcription or report of the interview is stored on a computer file and, as noted earlier, it is recommended that it be divided into chunks, or data items, each labelled so that, if separated from the rest of the interview report in the process of analysis, it can be easily identified and tracked back to source.

When taking notes during an interview it is worth deciding beforehand whether the respondent is to see the notes as they are made (by sitting next to the researcher) or not (by sitting face-to-face). In case study research it is often possible to interview a respondent a second time and this may enable questions to be refocused following a first round of analysis.

There are many variants of the standard face-to-face interview. Questionnaires are one, where the respondent is given written questions and asked to respond at his leisure. If the setting is one in which the researcher and respondent know each other this can be a successful strategy – but, of course, it lacks the interplay of an interview. Telephone interviews are another approach – particularly useful where access is a problem. In the research reported in Chapter 8, three questions were given on a sheet of paper to four groups of teachers, each group with tape recorder and a half-hour tape, and they were asked to record their discussion. (Was this asking questions or observing events?) It helped to tease out the ideology of the project being evaluated.

Observing events and noting carefully what happens

Like interviews, observation of educational events has a sense of formality. The actors know that they are being watched. Some behave as though there were no outsider present, some are on edge throughout, some 'play to the gallery' and some forget. The personal skills of the researcher are important in terms of putting the actors at their ease and her cognitive skills are important in selecting and noting significant aspects of the event.

Compared to interviews, events are less likely to be recorded on tape. Video work can be a problem because it entails pointing the camera at someone and thus making it clear that he or she is being directly observed. For this reason many classroom researchers, for example, prefer to make notes on a clipboard pad, sometimes augmented by an audio recording. The classroom observations reported in Chapter 9 were based on notes and audio tape, with the teacher wearing a small tape recorder and switching it on for agreed periods of the day.

What is noted depends, of course, upon what research question has been posed. Thus,

How often do the children in this classroom in a writing period ask their teacher for the spelling of a word and how often do they consult a dictionary?

will probably entail the researcher using a seating plan of the classroom and a two-way tally system, and probably surveying the whole class throughout the period. On the other hand,

How do the children work in this classroom in a writing period?

could involve the researcher in a routine of sitting with a group of children for three minutes, writing notes in a corner of the room for about three minutes and then going to another group. What she writes will depend on her knowledge and experience of children writing.

As with interviews, the report of the observation is stored on a computer file and divided into labelled data items.

A variant on observation reported by the researcher is observation reported by an actor in the research. For example, this could be a teacher's own diary of classroom events, written or taped, and passed to the researcher.

Reading documents

In terms of data collection, this means transferring significant quotations from documents to the research computer, ensuring that they are properly labelled as to source and treating each as a data item. It may seem tedious to type out something that is already printed, but if it is likely to feature in the case report it is worth doing at the outset.

Data analysis

In the first part of the chapter, in the discussion of stages of case study research, the concept of 'analytical statements' was introduced, and it was shown how first these might be in the form of summaries of answers to each research question, and then how they might focus on the original issue or problem or hypothesis of the research.

This led, in the hypothetical example of a theory-seeking case study, to a search for cause-and-effect explanations which could be tested against the collected analytical statements as well as the data items and then to an interpretation of which were significant. Finally, a fuzzy generalization was envisaged. Alternatively, if the case study had been of the story-telling, pic-ture-drawing or evaluative kind, the analytical statements themselves might have provided the framework for the report.

No doubt it all sounds rather complicated. Fundamentally what it is about is an intellectual struggle with an enormous amount of raw data in order to produce a meaningful and trustworthy conclusion which is supported by a concise account of how it was reached. Every enquiry is unique and so any attempt to generalize on analytical methods is a problematic venture, but Figure 7.1 is an attempt to pull these ideas together.

Word processors have made a tremendous difference to this kind of work with their facilities for copy, paste and sort, and there are available commercial programs which can be helpful if there is a very large amount of raw data to handle.

Writing case reports

Research reports often read as though the researchers knew from the start exactly what they were setting out to do and moved in a linear direction towards that end. This is called 'structured reporting'. Actual research is rarely like this, but it is a recognized convention that reports may be written in this way. The merit of the approach is that the reader can take a short cut through the meanderings taken by the researchers, get quickly to the essence of the claim to knowledge and learn how it was substantiated. It is particularly suited to research leading to fuzzy generalizations. Major alternatives are narrative reporting, in which the researcher tells the story of the research, more or less as it was, and descriptive reporting, in which the researcher draws a 'picture' of what has been discovered. Each of these is now described.

Structured reporting

Chris Holligan's theory-seeking case study report in Chapter 2 is an example of a structured report. It starts with an introduction which indicates what the report is about and who funded it. Second comes the conceptual background, which gives the local context of the enquiry, briefly reviews some of the relevant literature and refers to the political interest in the issue. Third is an account of the data collection. Then comes the data analysis, in two sections, where the second arises from the findings of the first. This leads to a statement of the empirical findings of the research and an interpretation of these, which is related to aspects of the literature cited earlier. Finally, two fuzzy propositions are put forward.

It is noteworthy that this is a very short report, whereas Holligan's case record of the research is 180 pages long – and this does not include the transcripts of the 40 two-hour interviews. There were a few issues other than the value of Educational Studies raised in the interviews, but the significant aspects of the research are in the short paper. This is typical of the experience of case study researchers: enormous effort goes into preparing short end points.

Figure 7.1 From research questions to empirical findings and case reports

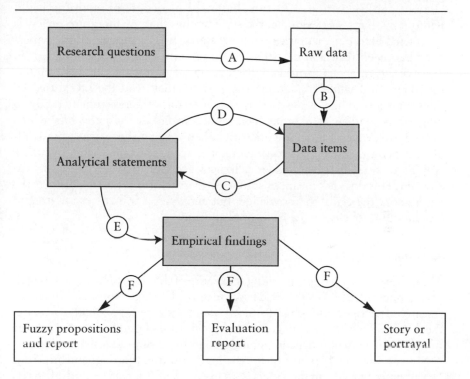

A Research questions, through interviews, observations and readings etc., lead to raw data.

B Raw data are stored in the case record as data items, each with a locatable reference.

C Creative and reflective thinking about the data items leads to draft analytical statements.

D The draft analytical statements are tested against the data items, and amended or discarded as necessary. C and D together are an iterative process aimed to get the most from the data.

E When the iterative process is exhausted the analytical statements are re-expressed as empirical findings.

F The empirical findings may lead to fuzzy propositions in a report, or to an evaluative report, or to a story or portrayal according to the type of educational case study. In each of these, sufficient of the data items and analytical statements will be included, with an account of the methodology, to give confidence in the report.

The shaded boxes all feature in the case record; everything, including draft copies of the reports, should be in the archive.

Other headings often used in structured reports include Method, Conclusions and Discussion. This time-hallowed procedure of reporting is not without its snags. For example, the style implies that the literature review is completed before the empirical enquiry starts. It is as though all the papers cited had been read and digested before the investigation was planned. In practice this rarely happens. People start a piece of research because it interests them, and while conducting the enquiry they read the literature. An important advantage of the style is that it enables the researchers easily to omit parts of their work that have ended in cul-de-sacs: the bits which proved irrelevant, or did not work, or could not be finished in the time available. It permits researchers to organize the account of the events in such a way as to present to the reader a logical account of what has been discovered. This does not mean, of course, that structured reporting distorts the truth about the claim to knowledge, but simply that it involves an attempt to communicate clearly the basis of that claim.

Narrative reporting

The narrative style of report writing tells more of the story of how the research was conducted. It gives the reader an idea of the stages through which the research developed and what decisions were made, but, in consequence, has the disadvantage of being long. But the significance of the claim to knowledge of the report may well depend upon the report carrying extensive evidence.

My account in Chapter 8 of the evaluation of the Nottinghamshire Staff Development Project in the 1980s is an example of a narrative study. It starts with an introduction which describes the project and what the aims of the Nottinghamshire LEA were in setting it up, and indicates the expected scope of the evaluation. The headings of Section 1 give a strong sense of a story unfolding:

> The beginning of the project
> Schools uncertain as to what they had embraced
> The road to Damascus
> What did the CSDCs learn at Eaton Hall?
> A hypothesis as to the ideology of the project
> Testing the hypothesis
> What did the headteachers make of the project?
> Redrafting the statement of the project's ideology

Stories have beginnings and ends. This one says:

> Some stories end happily: this is not the case here. Storm clouds were gathering. National government was attacking local government. The money ran out . . . the senior staff in the LEA moved to other jobs in other places. The Nottinghamshire Staff Development Project disappeared.

Stories may also carry moral messages. The final words of this one are a strong polemic:

> Perhaps the story hasn't ended yet. There are important messages for the national government, which has now gone beyond the National Curriculum (telling teachers what to teach) to the National Literacy Project (and soon the National Numeracy Project) which tells them how to teach. My dissident's concern has become reality: classrooms are being seen as units of production and teachers as technicians carrying out tightly defined functions. I believe it is time that the banner be raised again to assert the essentiality of teachers being recognized as professionals, fundamentally working for the effective education of young people and striving to enhance their practice through the shared process of structured reflective action. Only when they are free to exercise their own judgements and make their own decisions can they provide that enthusiasm, insight and enlightenment which young people need from their teachers if they are to grow up responding creatively and happily to a changing and challenging world.

The justification for such a statement lies in the detail of the report.

Narrative writing is usually best organized in sections in order to help the reader. Each section probably represents a period of time during which a significant stage of the research was conducted. The sections appear in chronological order and so stage-by-stage the report can show how questions were asked and answers sought, and how hypotheses were tested, found wanting, modified, retested and so on, while issues may be seen to develop and be refocused in the light of interim findings. A narrative account of research contains the same elements as a structured report, but instead of teasing these out and writing about each separately, data collection, analysis and interpretation are intermingled. Although this is the easiest style to write, it is a difficult style to write well. Essentially it is about writing true stories and, as with all story writing, the interest of the audience needs to be held: so, as in structured writing, it may be necessary to decide what to leave out of the total chronology of the research.

The case report in Chapter 8 of the evaluation of the Nottinghamshire project covers 20 pages: the evaluation report submitted to the LEA, which in effect was the case record plus seven pages of summative findings, was 295 pages long.

Descriptive reporting

The descriptive style of report writing draws a picture in words of something tangible: a classroom, a school, a system. As a form of case study reporting, it is based on careful probing and thoughtful analysis.

Stenhouse (1985: 52) described this as 'portrayal reporting'. He wrote:

'Portrayal reporting is an attempt to preserve some of the qualities of narrative in descriptive writing that lacks a natural story line. As in documentary film, characters, incidents, and descriptions of an environment in which they are set are juxtaposed to provide a portrayal which is interpetative of the case as a whole.' He also suggested that the term 'vignette' should be used for the short descriptive pieces that authors sometimes call 'case studies' and insert in their writing to illustrate particular points. On this he wrote: 'Vignette reporting has the status of a sketch compared to a fully worked picture. The selection of the subject of a vignette is an interpretative act, for a vignette crystallises some important aspect of a case' (Stenhouse 1988: 52).

An example of a picture-drawing case report, by Sheila Hall, is given in Chapter 10. The centrepiece of this extract from her report is a letter ('Dear Emma') from a student on final teaching practice to a friend, telling about the experience. It gives a vivid description of what it feels like: hopes, fears, satisfactions and worries. It is a piece of fictional writing (see below) arising from interviews with five students on their final teaching practice.

Zeller (1995: 76) has written a helpful account of the uses of narration and description in the writing up of case studies. She wrote:

> Narration provides a sense of immediacy of an event unfolding before the reader's eyes. The writer provides many details that capture the reader's interest; but, more importantly, the events, the story, or the characters exist in a world whose clock is ticking. Description, a type of writing normally used to convey how something may be apprehended through the senses, engages the reader's interest by providing interesting details. Description also enables the writer to display the events, story or characters against a particular setting – a place, culture, a set of norms. Narration can be a total organising strategy, subsuming or absorbing descriptions, scenes, and summaries . . . Description is a supporting strategy, rarely appearing in its pure form, but often intertwined with scenes and summary to support narration . . . Often there are sounds, smells and most importantly, sights that will help the reader understand the research setting and give the sense of being there. Descriptive passages within the research report will enrich its texture and contribute generally to a better understanding of the case.

Fictional reporting

Fictional names of people and places are often used in case study reports to give anonymity to the sources while retaining the human touch. But this is not the same as fictional reporting.

The 'Dear Emma' letter referred to above, which features in Chapter 10, is an example of fictional writing which draws together the findings of five interviews into one compact report. The reports of the five interviews are now lost, but the analysis of those interviews, in which 10 analytical statements (as featuring in the letter) were devised, is five times as long as the letter itself. This analysis is given in Chapter 10 and constitutes a justification for the substance of the letter. The fictional letter was discussed with the five students after the practice when they were back in college, and they agreed that the letter 'rang true' in representing the views of students on final teaching practice. As is noted in Chapter 10, this letter is one of four 'Dear Emma' letters, which gave an ongoing account of the fictional teacher's experience as she progressed from final teaching practice to her first week as a teacher, the end of her first year, and five years into her teaching career. The justification for this form of writing was this:

> The fictionalized form of presentation was used for three reasons: it enabled several accounts to be condensed into one, it permitted potentially defamatory statements to be delocalized, and, it is hoped, it grasped the reader's attention. It also enabled us, in the four letters to Emma, to change cross-sectional data, from three different generations of student teachers, into a simulated longitudinal account of one person's experience.
>
> (Chapter 10)

Fictional reporting is very demanding: it requires very thorough underpinning, and demonstration of this, by research.

Making a claim to knowledge and writing an abstract

The essential feature of any research report is that it makes a claim to knowledge and it is a well established and valuable practice to state that claim in the abstract of the report. A claim to knowledge may:

- contribute incrementally to the accumulated knowledge of the topic under study;
- challenge existing theoretical ideas;
- offer significant improvements to existing practice;
- give new insights into policy;
- introduce a new methodology of potential power;
- provide a 'significant piece in a jigsaw of understanding';
- bring together disparate findings and integrate them into a new theoretical structure.

The abstract should convey to the reader concisely and accurately within the space of a few sentences, the claim to knowledge that the authors are making. It should indicate the boundaries of space and time within which the enquiry has occurred. If there is a claim to generality, fuzzy or otherwise, this should be included. There should also be reference to the method of enquiry. Journals and thesis regulations usually put a limit of around 200 to 300 words to the length of an abstract.

The abstract should be a condensation of the substance of the paper, not a trailer or an introduction. 'Trailer' is a term borrowed from the cinema industry to describe a showing of a few highlights in order to win an audience. An 'introduction' tells that something is coming, but does not reveal its substance. These are not what is needed.

Abstracts are recycled in abstract journals and electronic networks and provide the main vehicle for other researchers to become aware of particular studies. Hence the more clearly they convey the claim to knowledge of the original paper the more useful they are in helping the reader to decide whether it is worth taking the trouble to obtain and read the original and possibly cite it in his or her own writing.

Both the abstract and the paper should make sense without the other.

Polemics

One of the prime reasons for doing any kind of research, and certainly for investing the enormous amount of time that case study research requires, is that one has personal interests and concerns about the subject of the research. As Barry Troyna (1995: 403) put it: 'all research, from its conception through to the production of data, its interpretation and dissemination, reflects a partisanship which derives from the social identity and values of the researcher.'

There are different views among researchers on this. My position is in agreement with Troyna. I believe that researchers should try to reveal their 'social identity and values' and to this end I see no difficulty in making polemical statements: for example, as part of the ending of a report. But it should be clear who is making the statement and that it is an expression of value and not of fact, thereby locating the polemic firmly within an ethic of respect for truth and respect for persons.

Audit certificate

Lincoln and Guba (1985: 318–27) give a detailed account of the suggestions made by Halpern for conducting an audit. Thirteen years later I am not aware of educational researchers taking these ideas seriously. This is regrettable and is probably owing not to the idea of audit being inappropriate, but to the suggested procedures being too complicated. I suggest a procedure which is much simpler.

Once the case report is written, a professional colleague is asked by the researcher to spend a few hours reading the report, and sampling parts of the case record in relation to the report. Key questions for the auditor could be:

1 What *claim to educational knowledge* is made, as expressed in the abstract?
2 Is the *conceptual background* given by the author appropriate?
3 Was the *collection of data*, as reported, appropriate, sufficient, ethical?
4 Was the *analysis and interpretation of data*, as reported, appropriate, sufficient, ethical?
5 Does the evidence of the report, as examined in answer to questions 2 to 4, *substantiate the claim to knowledge* made in answer to 1?

Alternatively the auditor could use the kind of analysis given at the end of Chapter 2 for Chris Holligan's case study.

Suppose that the auditor gave the author a simple statement of audit to publish with the case report. It might, for example, be like either of these:

> In terms of the evidence provided in this paper it is my professional judgement that the conclusions are based firmly on the data collected and the enquiry has been conducted according to the ethical guidelines of the British Educational Research Association.
> signed A. B. Smith, 1 June 1998

> The previous version of this paper has been modified by the authors in the light of my critique and the conclusions are now firmly based on the data collected, but anyone using the results is advised to consider carefully the extent to which the teachers being interviewed were able to give cogent answers to the questions put to them.
> signed C. D. Brown, 1 June 1998

Notes

1 The forms of ethical statements used here are taken from my *Creating Education through Research* (Bassey 1995: 15–16).
2 Keeves (1985), for example, lists these forms of validity: concurrent, construct, content, convergent, criterion-related, external, internal and predictive validity.
3 Lincoln and Guba describe positivist researchers as 'rationalists' and interpretive researchers as 'naturalists'.
4 In writing this account of trustworthiness, I am well aware that few of the researchers who currently prepare case studies embrace all eight of these questions. So I have to confess to a measure of normative advocacy in this section.

Part II | Examples of case studies

Preamble to Part II

The three case reports given here illustrate some of the features of case study made in the book.

'**The Nottinghamshire Staff Development Project 1985–1987**' is a story-telling case study about both formative and summative evaluation. Data collection was mainly by (a) recorded structured discussions in groups, (b) documents, (c) recorded interviews and (d) questionnaires. A hypothesis arose during the formative evaluation and was tested.

'**Classroom organization in primary schools**' is a story-telling case study about three theory-seeking case studies and a theory-testing survey. Data collection was mainly by (a) classroom observation and (b) interviews. The three case studies lead to a fuzzy proposition and this is then tested and leads to a fuzzy generalization.

'**What it is like to be a student on final teaching practice**' is a picture-drawing case study of fiction based on fact. Data collection was by interview. The fiction is supported by both internal and external tests of trustworthiness.

These case studies are long. This is evidence that there was prolonged engagement with data sources and persistent observation of emerging issues, as discussed in Chapter 7. It is hoped that the accounts are sufficiently detailed to give the reader confidence in the findings. The studies were time-consuming to prepare. All of this is a reminder to the would-be case study researcher that the path ahead is long, arduous and, as the Prayer Book says of marriage, not to be embarked on lightly.

8 | The Nottinghamshire Staff Development Project 1985–1987: a story-telling case study about an evaluation

Abstract

This is an account of the evaluation of an LEA project designed to develop the quality of teaching in Nottinghamshire schools. Its ideology was identified as: (1) all teachers are professional equals, irrespective of seniority; (2) all teachers can improve their classroom performance; (3) all teachers should have an intrinsic desire to improve their classroom performance; (4) the hierarchic structure of a school is not the instrument to direct the professional development of individual teachers, in terms of improving classroom performance; (5) professional development, in terms of striving to improve classroom performance, should be under the control of the individual teacher; (6) staff engaged in promoting professional development should only work with individual teachers on the basis of freely made contracts about the ownership of data which arises in any appraisal of the teacher's professional needs. This ideology was found to engender considerable enthusiasm among teachers in their professional work. The evaluation was conducted mainly by interview, study of documents, and recorded discussion in groups. The story carries an important message for today's national government that teachers can improve their professional work through ownership of their own development.

Introduction

In the summer of 1985, Nottinghamshire LEA obtained a substantial grant from the Manpower Services Commission to run a training programme for school and college teachers: this was first known as TRIST[1] but a year later became called the Nottinghamshire Staff Development Project (NSDP) when external funding was no longer available and the LEA funded it from its own resources.

The LEA defined the aim of the project as 'development of the quality of teaching', and saw it as a combination of staff development and curriculum development. Prior to starting the project the LEA had formally stated its intention 'to enhance the quality of learning' in its schools and colleges and this project represented a part of the LEA strategy towards that end.

The LEA gave responsibility for initiating and organizing the project to Dr Chris Saville (then principal inspector) and Mr Ray Shostak (then staff inspector). Mr John Pearce (a deputy headteacher) was seconded for a two-year period to be project coordinator and Mr Shostak became project director.

In September 1985 a first cohort of 17 secondary schools and four further education (FE) colleges began working on the programme. Each institution was allocated sufficient funds to allow replacement for the equivalent of one member of staff throughout the year. Over the three terms of the year, five members of staff could be seconded to the project in the following way. In the first term one senior member of staff took the role of 'Curriculum and Staff Development Coordinator' (CSDC) and was seconded to the project full-time for the complete term. In the second and third terms four other members of staff were seconded to the project full-time for half-term periods in which they engaged in one of the training modules. These modules were: 'Active learning methods', 'Assessment and course design', 'Multicultural education' and 'Technical and vocational education within the curriculum'.

The training of the CSDCs, and of the teachers taking the modules, started with a period of residence at the LEA's INSET centre, Eaton Hall, and continued in their own schools with report-back sessions at Eaton Hall. It was made clear that the teachers taking part in the project were expected to continue to pursue developments in school and college after their periods of secondment. The outline of the training programme was devised by Saville, Shostak and Pearce and the LEA invited tenders from selected institutions for provision of various modules within the programme.

In September 1986 a second cohort of six primary schools, 19 secondary schools and five FE colleges began the programme.

In October 1985 I was commissioned to evaluate the project. The evaluation was to be 'formative and responsive in style at two levels: an immediate level in which it should contribute to reflective action . . . and a future level in which it should contribute to reflection in the planning of the programme for future cohorts of schools'. I was then Reader in Education at Trent Polytechnic and well known in a number of Nottinghamshire primary schools as a researcher and as a teacher education tutor, but with no recent contacts with local secondary schools or FE colleges. I spent about 60 working days on the evaluation, employed a full-time secretary over the 21 months and had the assistance of a number of colleagues in conducting some of the interviews. I was particularly fortunate in being able to invite Dr Helen Simons (then at the Institute of Education, London, now professor at the University of Southampton) to join the Evaluation Advisory Committee.

I submitted four interim reports, as formative evaluations, and then in July 1987 a final report, as my summative evaluation. That document, 295 pages long, serves as the case record from which this story is told. (References to the case record are cited as 'CR', followed by a page number.) The story focuses on my attempts to understand and express the ideology of the instigators which underpinned the project, the enthusiasm which it generated and some of the issues which would affect future cohorts.

Section 1

The beginning of the project

It was clear from the start that this Nottinghamshire project was different from the usual type of in-service provision. It was intended eventually to reach all the LEA's schools and colleges. Institutions, not individuals, were being invited to participate. It entailed up to five teachers from each school or college being seconded for periods of a term or half-term. About a third of the secondment was spent at a residential centre, the rest in school working with colleagues. During the latter period the seconded teachers were expected to interact with their colleagues in confidential classroom observation and non-judgemental appraisal. The project was being led by senior members of the LEA with guidelines that seemed on the one hand autocratic and on the other democratic. And it was going to cost a lot of money. What was the thinking underlying it?

On 9 September 1985, 21 Nottinghamshire senior teachers from 21 secondary schools and FE colleges met at Eaton Hall International and began training: they were seconded to the project for the term and would be working part of the time together at Eaton Hall and the rest in their schools or colleges. These had responded to an invitation to participate from the LEA, expressed in these terms: 'each institution will be required to identify a senior member of staff to take part in the CSDC training programme with the undertaking that the new role will form part of its senior management structure' (*Nottinghamshire TRIST Draft Information Booklet* August 1985: 9 (CR 32)). The booklet described the LEA's intentions in some twenty pages. Under the heading of 'Programme design', it said:

This project focuses on the implementation of a delivery of enhanced classroom experience to pupils and students. The project is intended to build within its structure both the advantages of systematic development as well as current understanding of curriculum and professional growth in educational institutions. As noted earlier it begins with the concept of a 'Curriculum and Staff Development Consultant' and is rooted within the conceptual map of curriculum and professional development within the Authority.

(Ibid.: 8 (CR 32))

The conceptual map was a rather tattily sketched flowchart (CR 33) which shows appraisal leading to professional guidance and counselling as a central activity which might lead to either curriculum and professional development or to a variety of career changes. It also includes the cyclical idea of review leading to challenge and support and further review.

On 13 November I collected evidence from the 21 CSDCs. I was able to divide them into four groups (on a self-chosen basis) and asked each group on their own to spend half-an-hour discussing three questions and to provide me with a tape recording of the discussion. The questions were:

Is the work so far serving the project aim?
What contradictions are there in the work?
What issues deserve detailed evaluative study?

The case record contains 27 pages of transcript of these four group discussions (CR 70–107).

Schools uncertain as to what they had embraced

It is clear from a number of comments that the booklet issued by the LEA (described as a 'draft') had successfully encouraged schools to enlist in the project and put forward the name of a CSDC, but had remained obscure on the project's fundamental thinking about staff development, with the result that a tension had sometimes developed between the CSDC and the other senior managers of the school.

This conversation in one group makes the point about lack of intelligibility:

A: I found that the draft which they sent us through the post was very difficult to understand simply because I didn't understand the language they were using. I mean I read the words but they didn't mean anything.
B: I think for future reference a drastic revision of the written material –
C: Yes, and that might be a point for the evaluation, that it be couched in language which is not obscure. (CR 78)

Twenty minutes later this was said in the same group:

D: I am concerned that there is a philosophical mismatch between the aims of TRIST and the aims of the school and I think the original material that went into school wasn't clear enough for people to actually understand what TRIST was about. (CR 103)

Another group talked about related concerns on the gaps between the project and the schools' understandings of it:

E: It might be worth looking at a contradiction which may exist in that we are offering what we call 'a bottom-up' model. To what extent is it perceived as such by those with whom we are working?

F: I think that an issue which will definitely emerge with some ferocity is the idea that the present hierarchical structure with its concentration of power is going to be exposed if real staff curriculum development is to take place. (CR 104)

In a third group members made similar points:

G: I begin to discern, though not necessarily for me personally, that CSDCs are now back in institutions which do not have clear understandings of what TRIST is about, despite our efforts . . .

H: I agree with you on the identification of this issue . . . If we don't have some shared understanding of the project at senior management level I think that it will have little success in the rest of the school.

I: The issue I would like to raise concerns the transfer of TRIST from being in the ownership of the individual CSDC to becoming part of the corporate identity of the school as expressed in its aims, structure and procedures. (CR 107)

There was sufficient triangulation of evidence for me to suggest, in my first formative evaluation report, 'that the Nottinghamshire TRIST Information Booklet be rewritten, (a) in simpler language and more briefly, and (b) making overt the management-of-change ideology of Notts TRIST' (CR 37). But what was this ideology? Before trying to answer that question it is worth establishing the fact that something vital, powerful, exciting and sometimes disturbing happened to that first cohort of seconded teachers between 9 September when they started and 13 November when my tape recorders took evidence from them.

The road to Damascus

One group discussed as a contradiction the gap that they perceived between themselves and their colleagues when they returned to school because of their 'conversion' to the TRIST ideology.

P: I found my credibility questioned. Somebody, when I was very fervent about this thing on TRIST, said I was worse than a Jehovah's witness.

R: Somebody said exactly the same to me.

P: Yes they said it's exactly as though you've seen the light. (Laughter)

Well it really pulled me up in my tracks because I realized I was, I had undergone a certain conversion and I was speaking with some sort of light in my eyes. Then I realized that it was not really achieving the project aims, so I turned it down – I turned it down a lot then.

R: Yes, I did exactly the same.

Q: I had this concern of credibility and also the Damascus road job you were referring to. I think all of us went through it, and I think it shows in the enthusiasm with which other people are planning and the crossing over of boundaries perhaps they wouldn't normally cross over.

P: A thing most people said about me was that I had changed considerably as a person as a result of four weeks up here. My going away has changed the whole dynamic of the management.

R: This is the crux for me. Most of the management team have threatened to send me back to Eaton Hall so many times now, I wonder whether I dare go in a room with them. I mean I've become such a challenge to them, it's ridiculous. (Laughter)

P: Well I'm seen as a challenge, I'm seen as devaluing the work that's gone on.

R: Yes.

P: I'm seen as a destroyer of policies which I've previously supported. I don't think that they were the right way to do things and the annoying thing is I appear to have an inner strength which they can't –

R: Oh my God this is worrying me now. (Laughter)

P: Well this is how it seems to other people. You're untouchable. (Laughter) One said to me, 'I wish I could become a Tristite'. (CR 75)

Later in this discussion, S raised a question about readiness to take on board the TRIST ideology.

S: I guess I'm worried by this road to Damascus stuff. I mean –

R: Well I'd love to know about it.

S: – if somebody else on the senior management team had come on this would they have come back with the same sort of fervour. No, I can't imagine that any of the others would.

R: Absolutely, because I don't believe that any externally imposed course like TRIST was, can actually change a person that much. You know we can only be encouraged from where we were, so that you've been encouraged from where you were at the point that you came.

S: Certainly many people would never have come on this course anyway.

R: That's the first thing –

S: Yes, yes.

R: – by actually coming you showed a predilection –

S: But that only works for those people who volunteered to come, what about all those who were pushed out to come?

R: Well then I suspect that they're still fairly well where they were.

Not everyone found their schools receptive, but support could be provided by other teachers on the project, as this extract from another group discussion shows.

D1: Can I refer back to our conversation this morning D4?

D4: Yes.

D1: I could see that you were not your normal self – and then we had a beer together (laughter) and what I said to you appeared to help you because it had helped me enormously. Back on the patch I felt the need to have somebody with whom I could personally talk about what I was doing in a detached sort of way; somebody who would help me to evaluate what I'm doing . . . I think this feeling of isolation you've got –

D4: You helped me considerably.

D1: – is something that I was afraid of because I am senior management.

D4: Having sat through lunch and walked down the lane, I have decided that the only person who can fulfil that role in my school is the head, and whether he likes it or not, he is going to be told that that is what I expect of him and if he fails me then TRIST is floundering in his school! He volunteered his school to take part in the TRIST project! I think it is the only way I can succeed and you can tell I'm determined by my tone of voice.

D2: I thought you were speaking for the benefit of the evaluator.

D4: No I wasn't.

D3: For you there was obviously a very severe contradiction in what you were doing.

. . .

D2: Your problem seems to be with the head.

D4: Yes. The head is burying his head: he doesn't want to know; he avoids me; he won't speak to me; he won't talk about TRIST. I might rock the boat; I might disturb things. He doesn't really want to know; he didn't really want the school to be involved; he allowed it to go in very reluctantly.

D2: If I can pull something through for the tape recorder,[2] what you seem to be saying (and this might be a reflection of other people, not just you) is that your institution has got itself involved in the project when the head doesn't really feel that the involvement is worth a candle.

D4: That is exactly what I am saying.

D2: And your next action plan, if I can put it that way, is that you're going to confront him with this problem and get some reaction from him one way or another?
D4: Yes. (CR 95–6)

What did the CSDCs learn at Eaton Hall?

Pointers to the ideology of this project can be found in three of the training modules taken by the CSDCs during their first residential period at Eaton Hall.

Module A focused on the skills of working in groups. Some of the issues considered are illustrated by these extracts from documents discussed by them.

- Many of the learning environments we create for teachers, both inside school and outside, involve working in groups. These range from the very formal meeting to the more informally tasked group. It is possible to make meetings work more productively for us by learning more of their development. *Working in Groups 1* (CR 36)
- Does the group need a chairperson? If yes – what will be the role and who will be the chairperson? Do we need a group process observer? How will we handle areas of disagreement? *Contracting the Group* (CR 36)
- Autocratic style: does anyone attempt to impose his will or values on other group members or try to push them to support his decision? *Working in Groups 2* (CR 36)

In the countryside calm of Eaton Hall this was unemotive, unexceptional stuff. But in the rapid decision-making action of schools it could be seen as a challenge to those who perceived themselves to be in authority.

Module B was entitled 'Helping skills' and included sessions on aspects of counselling such as challenging, empathy and problem management. This was used to underpin the concept of *structured reflective action* for the appraisal of teacher performance leading to teacher development.

> This is based on a process model of operation in that there is a recognition that 'solutions' to professional problems evolve through a personal process of structured reflective action . . . an approach which involves negotiation, the structured informing of practice, the establishment of criteria of performance and the focus on skills and professional attributes . . .
> Implementing such an approach in itself requires the acquisition and development of a set of helping skills and a framework into which these skills can be deployed . . . it offers a model that enables the helper to work in a positive way to help others take action to help themselves.
> *(Helping Skills 1* (CR 37))

This extract from one of the group discussions shows that this process began quickly when the CSDCs returned to their schools and colleges.

E: I've been able to talk to two members of staff. Both have asked me to do specific tasks which are directly going to affect the quality of their teaching, and indeed their understanding. One phrase from Module B that has come back to me again and again is 'you will be surprised at the enhancement in the quality of professional conversations which come out of this kind of work'. There is no question that philosophically I've got into deeper levels with staff than I've ever been able to do before . . .

F: When I got back to school I spent the first week or so simply talking to people very informally about TRIST as I know it. Since half-term I've started to talk to people in a more specific way about their work as teachers, themselves as professionals, and their future development. I'm not going to pretend that I've talked to many people and covered all three areas, but I've made a start. I find that in the first interview, let's say 35 minutes, they are more than happy to talk about their work as teachers and this is the first time that they've probably sat down in school and done that with anyone; and I find it absolutely fascinating that they, in every case, have welcomed the opportunity. But this is just the beginning isn't it?

G: Can we say then that the aim is being fulfilled, that we are actually improving the quality of teaching?

F: Well we're starting on the process, we need to establish the trust don't we? We need first to establish for our colleagues a way of thinking about themselves and their work, because many of them perhaps haven't ever done this before. And then when we start to talk about their work, we can begin to consider ways in which they as professionals can improve on their performance. But you can't do that quickly.

G: I think E is right there, that the quality of debate once it's removed from the day-to-day issues in a sense is much better. I'm not sure that the project aim is being fulfilled in one sense in that I've already done quite a lot of classroom observations and interviews but so many different issues are thrown up that I'm not sure where to go next. (CR 38)

Module C developed ideas for classroom observation in the context of 'teacher' and 'observer' being professional equals. A code of practice for action research evolved based on negotiated agreement between teacher and observer prior to any observation. This included:

- the precise purpose of and reason for the study;
- the scope, length and methods of study;

- the form, use and release boundaries of any report or record made during or after the observation;
- the confidentiality or subsequent use of materials and or data gathered during the observation. *Draft Code of Practice and Suggested Guidelines Governing Action Research in Schools* (CR 37)

There were other modules used in the CSDC initial training, but these three seem to have been the setting in which the CSDCs (or at least most of them) caught fire with the ideas which they described as 'Trist'. The starting point for the module presenters, and for the CSDCs, was a document called *The TRIST Programme: Ground Rules and Principles of Engagement for Curriculum and Staff Development Consultants*. It was issued to the CSDCs on their first day at Eaton Hall and subsequently they were invited to rewrite it. Key points were:

- The central purposes of the role of the CSDC are those of consulting, negotiating needs, appraising and facilitating . . .
- CSDCs do not have an automatic right of access to another teacher, his/her file, or his/her classroom. Access to a teacher is by negotiation through a contracted relationship . . .
- The role of CSDC is not judgemental except in a diagnostic sense . . .
- Information gathered from discussions with a teacher or from observations in a teacher's classroom is confidential to that teacher and may not be released without that teacher's permission. (CR 35)

A hypothesis as to the ideology of the project

In February 1986 I issued my first formative report as evaluator to the project. This recommended that the Information Booklet (which was about to be reissued to attract the next generation of participating schools) should be written in simpler language and more briefly, and should make overt the management-of-change ideology of the project. I described what I had learned about the ideology of the project, by which I meant 'a set of coherent beliefs which have become held fervently by a group of people in their attempt to give meaning to their work'. I put it like this:[3]

> This project is based on an ideology which sees teachers as professional equals irrespective of seniority. It is an ideology which recognises that teachers have strengths and weaknesses in the classroom; it asserts that everyone, however able, can improve in classroom performance; it also asserts that teachers have an intrinsic desire to change for the better. Coupling these three points together, the project ideology vigorously demands that change is under the control of the person who changes, hence the insistence on negotiation, contracting, and personal ownership of personal data.

A consequence of this ideology is that the hierarchic structure of a school is not seen as an instrument to direct the professional development of its teachers. That is the responsibility of the teachers themselves, individually and, within a society of professional equals, collectively.

(CR 35)

Testing the hypothesis

In February 1986 I sent a questionnaire to the CSDCs asking them to what extent they embraced the ideology of TRIST as I had identified it. Nineteen of the 21 replied. The following box gives both the form of the questionnaire and the number of responses in each category (CR 42).

To what extent have you embraced the TRIST ideology? These are features of the TRIST ideology which I have identified. Please indicate the extent to which at the present time you subscribe to them, by putting ticks in the appropriate boxes.

'Can't answer' implies that the issue is too complex to be answered by a 'tick in a box'.

	Strongly agree	Agree	Disagree	Strongly disagree	Can't answer
(a) All teachers can improve in classroom performance	14	2	1	0	2
(b) All teachers have an intrinsic desire to change for the better	2	4	8	0	5
(c) Professional development is the responsibility of the teachers themselves	4	3	6	0	6
(d) All teachers are professionally equals – irrespective of seniority	9	8	1	0	1
(e) The hierarchic structure of a school is not the instrument to direct the professional development of its teachers	8	9	0	0	2

The questionnaire included space for written comments. Items (b) and (c) were clearly the most contentious, and these responses suggest why (CR 44). Item (b):

- 'This is too sweeping. *Most* teachers do wish to do things well . . .' (Respondent 9)
- 'I now find this a complex question. Before TRIST I believed it. I now know that most colleagues do have that desire, but that the concept of "better" is not easily understood by all of my colleagues. Better for whom? TRIST's philosophy of the enhancement of learning as a qualitative aim is not for some staff the central issue: some remain very much engrossed in maintaining the status quo.' (Respondent 3)
- 'I think a majority of teachers have an intrinsic desire to change for the better, but some need more challenge/support.' (Respondent 14)

Item (c):

- 'As professionals, individuals have a responsibility for their development, based primarily on assessment of what their specific needs are. The school has a responsibility to provide appropriate opportunities and support. The LEA has a financial and practical duty to provide appropriately targeted INSET.' (Respondent 9)
- 'Responsibility for the professional development of teachers may lie within the teaching profession as a whole, or within the institution through a formal staff development policy etc. However, I cannot see how it can lie solely with an individual teacher since professional development must involve areas of guidance, counselling, support etc.' (Respondent 5)

As a result of these replies I made some modifications to my statement of the ideology, but before giving this I turn to what some of the headteachers said about the project. They were, of course, all volunteers who had put their schools forward in the light of the LEA's invitation to participate.

What did the headteachers make of the project?

Around the time that the questionnaire was sent to the CSDCs, nine of the heads and principals of the first cohort of participating institutions were interviewed. Among other questions they were asked what they saw as the main characteristics of the project. The interviews were taped and transcribed, and the transcripts 'tidied up' and sent to the interviewees for approval for publication in the report. These extracts focus on the issues of the ideology of the project and the responses of the participants.

Some heads, like this one, had a firm grasp of what the LEA officers who initiated the project had in mind.

> The main characteristics, as far as this school is concerned, are that it is a teacher-centred, teacher-based, teacher-initiated, and teacher-run professional development programme . . . the whole kit and caboodle belongs to teachers. That is not to say that I'm not a teacher or that the deputies aren't teachers, but the only way proper trust could ever have

been established between the consultant and her team and the staff room, is for the staff to believe that they are not going to come running here telling me what has been said. The CSDC has my ear, but I don't have her mouth, if you understand the metaphor . . . We have had other inservice training programmes here. They have been joined grudgingly by people and I don't know if anything has come out of them of any lasting value. There has been cynicism of the chalk-face worker and a suspicion that the people who aren't at the chalk-face may have fine ideas, but they go away at the end of the day and don't have to live with kids.

(CR 115)

He said that his only contribution to the project had been to write the school's submission to be involved. He went on to say: 'The enthusiasm of the people that have come back is quite extraordinary. One who came back this morning is still shocked, but quite breathless with excitement. The two previous teachers are rejuvenated people. The effects have been smashing on them . . . they have now found a new lease of life and a new meaning on what they are doing' (CR 116).

One head expressed the theme of the project as a 'grass roots' movement which might enable staff to become themselves the agents of change.

In my school I see it as a way of harnessing and developing enthusiasm for curriculum initiatives by skilling people at the grass roots, and tapping and developing their enthusiasm . . . As a contrast, in the past, staff development and INSET had a strong element of paternalism whereby those in management and those with particular skills tried to pass on their wisdom to the staff. This project will I hope enable staff at all levels to become themselves the agents of change.

(CR 120)

Another, who clearly recognized the value of the grass roots nature of the project, referred to the 'pain' of letting others discover for themselves what he felt he already knew.

Our previous staff development consisted of head, deputies, and heads of departments deciding what should be going on rather than giving an open-ended approach to individuals. It was very tidy and based on what we'd identified, whereas this is much more open-ended in terms of the kind of discussion that's going on. So far it brings the same answers but it frames them in a very interesting – if at the same time frustrating – way. People who haven't thought about where they're going, come back full of ideas and they're the sort of ideas one would have put to them anyway if we had had the chance. Of course it's more effective that they come and say it, but it's sometimes very painful to sit back and let them put over their thoughts!

(CR 126)

Not all the heads seemed to recognize the full intention of the approach. Thus, although the head quoted in this next extract referred to a 'bottom-up model', there is a sense of a hierarchic approach to staff development in what is said:

> The main characteristics of the project are: its focus upon the classroom, the impetus given to the vision of where the school wants to go in terms of staff and curriculum development, the skill awareness provided to move forward far more vigorously, and the general opening up of staff awareness that staff development has a high profile . . . There is no doubt that the staff concerned are enthusiastic, feel involved, are open-minded and able to operate in other teachers' classrooms. The programme has opened up staff attitudes generally towards looking at classroom experiences in a non-threatening manner. It is essentially a bottom-up model of development.
>
> (CR 122)

Redrafting the statement of the project's ideology

By March 1986, I felt sure that the LEA officers who instigated the project had a clear ideology, with which the first generation of CSDCs were either in full agreement or nearly so, and which was supported, sometimes with less accord, by the heads of the school involved. I modified my earlier view of it in the light of subsequent evidence and expressed it in these six statements:

1 All teachers are professional equals – irrespective of seniority.
2 All teachers can improve their classroom performance.
3 All teachers should have an intrinsic desire to improve their classroom performance.
4 The hierarchic structure of a school is not the instrument to direct the professional development of individual teachers, in terms of improving classroom performance.
5 Professional development, in terms of striving to improve classroom performance, should be under the control of the individual teacher.
6 Staff engaged in promoting professional development should only work with individual teachers on the basis of freely made contracts about the ownership of data which arises in any appraisal of the teacher's professional needs. (CR 46)

In the light of the evidence collected (of which only a small part has been given here), I reiterated my view, in a formative evaluation report dated March 1986, that the ideology should be made transparent to schools before they enlisted. I put it like this:

Notts TRIST has a clearly defined ideology and when teachers are seconded to the programme, either as CSDCs or as module participants, the instigators hope that these teachers will accept the tenets of the ideology and use it in subsequent work in their schools as the basis for promoting professional development among colleagues.

Suppose that an instrument is developed which can measure uptake of the ideology. Suppose that it is used not in a quantitative sense (there is little to be gained from ascertaining that someone is 55% a Tristite!), but in a qualitative sense. Suppose that it is used as an instrument which enables the individual to identify any tenets of the ideology with which he or she is unhappy, or uncertain. Rather than dismiss such, it is suggested that these should be recognised as the points for professional growth. Hence the advantage of identifying them is that they *are* brought to the surface and can be discussed and debated at length until the individual either takes them on board or becomes sure that this part of the TRIST ideology is not for him/her. It is envisaged that such an instrument would be used in conjunction with tutorials – which would serve as the arena for debate about the tenets of the ideology. These tutorials might be instigator-to-initiate, or initiate-with-fellow-initiate.

It is important to provide an escape route for initiates who find themselves out of sympathy with the ideology. They need to have effective opportunity to make an honourable withdrawal and return to their school or college to continue their erstwhile duties and, maybe, to be replaced by a colleague who will be in sympathy with the ideology of the project. This is important for them in their own right, as professionals who take a different stance on the development of teachers, but it is also important for the TRIST instigators, because it legitimates the process of initiating people into the TRIST ideology. It legitimates it as an *educational* process insofar as 'education' implies that something is learned with the full agreement of the learner.

[Here I put suggestions for the instrument, based on the six statements listed above.] It is envisaged that this instrument could be used with future CSDCs as well as participants in the modules. It may be that future cohorts of teachers in the TRIST programme will be less convinced from the start of the merits of the ideology. Possibly those schools and colleges which volunteered for the first cohort contained those who were already in the main committed to the ideology. If this proves to be the case it may be more important for a monitoring instrument to be available.

Underlying this report is the view that if one is trying to socialise people into an ideology, there is a need for an instrument to monitor the extent to which the socialising process is successful.

(CR 45)

Earlier in this report I had defended the idea of socializing into an ideology in these words:

> I do not consider that the instigators of Notts TRIST are trying to indoctrinate people into their ideology; they are not seeking blind subservience to its tenets, but a reasoned recognition of its value which leads to acceptance. Yes, the instigators do want people to adopt their ideology, but they are setting out to do this by rational persuasion, not emotional appeal. Initiation is being treated as an educational process . . . I take the process of socialising teachers into the TRIST ideology as legitimate in an educational and democratic sense.
>
> (CR 40–1)

This report was not well received by the project team. My guess is that it touched a raw nerve. They were unhappy with the idea that they had an ideology and that they wanted to socialize others into it: they preferred to think that they were part of a grass roots movement which was developing its ideas through the discourse of the CSDCs working in schools. They dismissed my report (the second of four formative reports), implying that it was not the kind of evaluation that was wanted. I discussed this with Helen Simons and in one powerful sentence she told me one of the great truths of evaluation: 'If your report is any good you can't expect the sponsors to love you for it.'

Section 2

Formative and summative evaluation

The evaluation study continued for another 15 months. After the disagreement with the project team I wrote this about formative and summative evaluation.

> Insights into the processes of evaluation can be gained through consideration of a train journey.
>
> Summative evaluation is carried out at the end of the journey. The evaluator meets the passengers at the terminus and asks questions of them as they climb off the train.
>
> In a positivist perspective the evaluator notes whether the train arrived on time and counts how many passengers completed the journey. A questionnaire is issued asking for a response in the form 'agree/disagree/don't know' to the statement 'I enjoyed the journey'. The report is addressed to the railway company and may be used by them to decide to close the line, change the schedule, or spend more on advertisements.
>
> However, if the summative evaluator works from an interpretive

perspective s/he asks about the experiences of the journey – what views the individual passengers saw, how comfortable they found the train, what new acquaintances were struck up, and whether the amenities of the train were adequate for them. The report of this kind of evaluation may be used by the railway company for the purposes of improving the facilities for passengers, and it may also be published in a travel magazine because of its general interest to travellers.

By contrast the formative evaluator needs to travel on the train, for the task is different. The concern is with the success of the specific journey. The questions asked may be similar to those posed by the interpretive summative evaluator, but the output from the evaluation needs to be immediate. If the windows are dirty or the carriages cold, the formative evaluator needs to point this out immediately. If some of the passengers are singing loudly and disturbing others the formative evaluator needs to tell them. Certainly these issues may have a bearing on the future programme of the railway company, but the formative evaluator's prime concern is with the passengers on the present journey.

(CR 17)

This served as a useful metaphor for expressing – in August 1986 – my concern that I couldn't provide the kind of formative evaluation that the project team was asking for.

With only 30 days scheduled for my evaluative work per year I haven't had time to travel on the journey with the passengers. All I have been able to do has been to meet some of them at railway stations along the line. But by the time I have processed the data collected from them, the train has gone further up the line. My findings are too late for immediate formative purposes. It is not just a matter of time; it is also a matter of methodology. Interviews and discussions have been painstakingly transcribed and edited to produce documents in which the inarticulations of the spoken word transcribed into the written word are eliminated. Interviews handled in this way have then been sent back to the interviewees for checking, to ensure that they have said what they meant to say. The technique has produced some deep and colourful accounts from TRIST participants of their experiences which, put together, offer reflective reports about what *has* happened. Also, hopefully, this has been done within an ethical framework which has ensured that nobody feels misrepresented nor uncomfortably exposed. But the production of such reports takes considerable time and, as a result, the train has left the station by the time they are ready!

Since I cannot 'travel on the train' I cannot provide immediate formative evaluation. But it has become clear over the year that this is actually being done effectively by the project co-ordinator and the various tutors. Their antennae are carefully tuned to the day-by-day experience of the participants and they respond quickly: they are, of course, 'travelling on the train'.

What is likely to be a more valuable approach for the evaluation is to see it as formative for the work of the next cohort. To this end I propose to conduct case studies in individual schools and colleges. Inevitably it means a limited sampling, but hopefully it will provide in-depth perspectives of value for the future. I was going to extend the metaphor by suggesting that I will be travelling in just a few compartments of the train and thus engaging in extended conversations with a few passengers – but the metaphor breaks down for it is unlikely that the compartments are all travelling in the same direction.

(CR 17–18)

Summative evaluation of the second cohort designed as formative for the third

In the second year of evaluation I worked with teachers of the second cohort of the project. I concentrated on two schools and one college in trying to assess the impact of the project on these institutions. The data were supplemented by one-off interviews in 12 schools and colleges, two questionnaires to the CSDCs and an interview with a 'dissident' – a teacher who took strong exception to the concept of the project.

The outcome was a set of 10 summative statements which I framed in April 1987 (CR 23–8). This is not the place to reiterate these, but reproducing a couple gives an indication of the potential value of this kind of evaluation. Each had a number of cross-references to evidence in the body of the report. This was the first:

> The project creates considerable enthusiasm in schools and colleges for staff development in terms of the Authority's definition of staff development as 'a planned process of development which enhances the quality of pupils learning by identifying, clarifying and meeting the individual needs of staff within the context of the institution as a whole'.

> (a) This enthusiasm is strongest in heads/principals, CSDCs and module attenders.
> (b) Enthusiasm is also strong in many of the people with whom CSDCs have worked in determining individual professional needs.
> (c) A proportion of staff (dependent on the size of the school/college, among other factors) is uncertain about the value of the project.
> (d) A small minority of staff treat the project with scepticism and cynicism.

This was a fairly obvious statement, but one which nevertheless I felt the LEA needed to have, in writing, as a justification for the expenditure on the project. It was supported by a large body of evidence that I had collected. These quotes from interviews are indicative of the support for the project:

> When W returned from her CSDC training at Eaton Hall she came back like a whirlwind. Before when people from school have been on courses, there has been no feedback into the school and the general feeling has been that attendance at courses is for personal purposes linked to one's own work and possibly to one's own prospects for promotion. The strong impression is that the Notts Staff Development Project is different.
>
> The Notts Staff Development Project has for the first time in my experience given teachers the opportunity to sit down with each other and discuss in detail what they are doing in their teaching. The most notable thing about staff training in the past has been its absence! Before this project there had been no serious attempt at staff training on a scale beyond that of the individual teacher.
>
> The NSDP is about members of staff having an opportunity to learn about staff development and pupil development and then returning to school to share the ideas with those who choose to take advantage of them . . . The project is concerned, as I see it, with non-judgmental appraisal for the purpose of improvement of practice . . . As a professional I take the view that one can never reach perfection, and never reach the ultimate in competence. There is always room for improvement – and this view seems fairly central to the project.
>
> (CR 3)

I had not met much opposition to the project, but an interview with one teacher (whom I labelled a 'dissident') put me in a dilemma. He had said:

> It seems to me that industrial managers perceive people as units of production: this is not the way educational managers should see teachers. I recognise that there are problems, at an intellectual level, in looking at teachers as professionals, but the important thing is that the self-ascribed status, or the way that people perceive themselves in teaching, is as professionals. Involved in that are questions of autonomy in the classroom. So strategies which are influenced by industrial techniques are not likely to work and are likely to produce alienation. I think this is a major problem in the relationships between teachers and the Authority. Educational management should be quite different from industrial management.
>
> (CR 259)

My dilemma was that I agreed with his views in every respect bar one: I was convinced that the authority was not working to the industrial model in this project. But I was in the role of evaluator, not protagonist, or even apologist.

I didn't argue with him but just tried to reproduce faithfully his views, and published them in the report as evidence of 'scepticism and cynicism'.

The other nine evaluative statements focused on issues which the evidence collected suggested the course team needed to address. Here I include one final example:

> There is inevitably a tension between the management function of a school/college and the development function (because of conflicting demands upon time). Creating a distance between the CSDC (as the agent of development) and the senior management team may be to the advantage of development in a large school or college, but may be to its disadvantage in a small school, for example a primary school.
>
> Interpersonal relationships provide the matrix on which goodwill and co-operation is based and these can be imperilled in a small school if the CSDC is distanced from the head by the nature of the project. In primary schools it is probably important that the staff as a whole act as a development team.
>
> In larger schools and colleges interpersonal relationships are equally important within the teams into which the school/college divides (such as senior management, department, faculty, etc.) but goodwill and co-operation between these teams depends in large part upon the flow of information and the opportunity to participate in decisions. Thus the creation of a 'staff development' team, distanced from the senior management team, may be advantageous in promoting development in a larger school or college, provided there is effective communication and agreement on decision making.
>
> Five people (one CSDC and four module attenders) is a strong starting point for a 'staff development' team in a larger school or college. On the other hand in a primary school it may be better to avoid the situation in which say five teachers become fully immersed in the project and one, two or three get left behind.

Sad ending

My contract ended in April 1987 and the final report was delivered to Nottinghamshire LEA in July 1987. Some stories end happily: this is not the case here. Storm clouds were gathering. National government was attacking local government. The money ran out because local management of schools – introduced in the 1988 Education Reform Act, required all LEAs to cut centrally funded projects and instead delegate nearly all of their funding to schools. Eaton Hall – the residential centre which had been the 'hot house' for the project – was closed. The senior staff in the LEA moved to other jobs in other places. The Nottinghamshire Staff Development Project disappeared.

Two aspects of the project now remain in the schools: the few hundred teachers who had become involved all took away, in some form or other, a renewed belief in their own professional abilities; and appraisal, required by national government, when introduced to Nottinghamshire was firmly cast in the mould of the NSDP with the appraisee in professional control, not the appraiser. The Notts Appraisal Scheme requires negotiated agreement between teacher and observer prior to any observation, and confidentiality in the discussions.

Perhaps the story has not ended yet. There are important messages for the national government, which has now gone beyond the national curriculum (telling teachers what to teach) to the national literacy project (and soon the national numeracy project) which tells them how to teach. My dissident's concern has become reality: classrooms are being seen as units of production and teachers as technicians carrying out tightly defined functions. I believe it is time that the banner be raised again to assert the essentiality of teachers being recognized as professionals, fundamentally working for the effective education of young people, and striving to enhance their practice through the shared process of structured reflective action. Only when they are free to exercise their own judgements and make their own decisions can they provide that enthusiasm, insight and enlightenment which young people need from their teachers if they are to grow up responding creatively and happily to a changing and challenging world.

Notes

1 In 1985/6 the project was known as TRIST (TVEI Related Inservice Training where TVEI stood for Technical and Vocational Education Initiative).
2 This illustrates the point that tape recorders can sometimes be a stimulus to participants expressing ideas.
3 There is an intuitive leap from the evidence to this formulation. The evidence given in this chapter so far is an attempt to portray for the reader the kind of data that I had collected. Working it through again, 10 years later, I have no reason to change what I then wrote (other than to drop the word TRIST, which a year later disappeared), but I still cannot explain the creative process which took me from the evidence to this hypothesis.

9 | Classroom organization in primary schools: a story-telling case study about three theory-seeking case studies[1] and a theory-testing survey

Abstract

This is an account of three case studies and a 779-teacher survey of primary classroom organization and curriculum management carried out in Nottinghamshire in the 1970s. The case studies were conducted by classroom observation and interview, and the survey by interview. These lead to the following fuzzy generalization: it is likely that the organization of most primary school classrooms can be described in terms of some or all of four major organizational strategies: classwork in one subject, groupwork in one subject, groupwork in several subjects and individual work (with the definitions given in the chapter). The case studies illustrate the author's view that before the Education Reform Act of 1988 and the subsequent and continuing interference of the state in classrooms, there were dedicated and competent teachers fully committed to the needs of the children in their care who were quite able to work effectively without official monitoring and state harassment.

Introduction

This is an account of studies[2] that I carried out in Nottinghamshire in the mid-1970s, now retold as a story to illustrate some of the features of case study which this book is about. I was a tutor in the Department of Education of Trent Polytechnic supervising students in primary schools and, at first not having direct teaching experience in that field, was trying to understand the various patterns of organization that local schools used. I was particularly

fascinated by the way that s[...]
one time, yet the children [...]
expected of them. How di[...]
students learn to do the same[...]
through a few case studies. [...]
four major organizational str[...]

I made a number of studies:[...]
classrooms, yet each was uniqu[...]
enced people who readily and[...]
chose them as teachers whom I[...]
cope with me observing in their[...]
when being watched and recorde[...]
that the descriptions given in the[...]
day practice of these teachers at [...]

I spent time with the teacher an[...]
to build up mutual understanding[...]
room and I obtained a list of the [...]ren were told
that I would be spending a day wit[...] and would be very busy writing –
so not to disturb me. During the day the teachers wore a tape recorder over
their shoulder, with a microphone on the shoulder strap, and switched it on
for 'organizational' events during the day at my request. I made notes
throughout the day on a clipboard. The focus was on how the teacher initiated, monitored and brought to a close the children's work, how the children
were grouped and what oral instructions the teacher used. Afterwards I had
a detailed conversation with the teacher, with the tape recorder running,
about the pattern of organization and the classroom rules. The case study
was then written (as the draft of what is presented here) and given to the
teacher within a few days of the event for checking for both trustworthiness
and acceptability to her or him. They all agreed to the cases being published.
Mrs W showed hers to her father and said that he was totally amazed at what
his daughter achieved in a day. I felt the same in each of these classrooms.

A day in Mrs M's classroom: a theory-seeking case study

General description

The school is on the outskirts of a small town in the East Midlands. The
buildings date from the nineteenth century and are aptly described by the
head as 'looking like a cow byre from the outside'. There are four classrooms, each with a high vaulted roof and brightly painted. There is no hall
and so assembly is held in one classroom and dinner is provided in another.
It is a separate infant school which feeds three different junior schools,
although most children go to just one of these. Transfer is in September
following the seventh birthday. Mrs M's classroom is 52 square metres in

...re large enough to make the room bright. ...s and a chair for each child. A woven mat to ...ed for class discussions and the children sit on it ...ort periods. There are 34 children in the class: they ...s M is 32. After three years of teaching she had a break ...nd returned to teaching a year and a half ago.

...dy

...0	Mrs M arrives and prepares for the morning's work.
9.00	The children come into the classroom and some show Mrs M things that they have brought: books, egg boxes etc. They sit on the mat at the centre of the room.

9.03   *Mrs M*: Let's see who's here. Grant?
Grant: Yes, Mrs M.
Mrs M: Shaun?
Shaun: Yes, Mrs M.
Mrs M: . . . My goodness. No one away. What do I put at the bottom of my register?
Children: Thirty-four.
The register and the collection of dinner money are used for extending number and language experience.
Mrs M: (Receiving a purse containing dinner money.) Thank you Elaine. A pound note is this? How much change?
Elaine: 25 pence.
Mrs M: Yes, 25 pence change. How many ten pences do I give Elaine? (to the class).
Children: One?
Mrs M: No. Two! And how many fives?
One. Yes. Two tens and one five.
There's your change, Elaine.
Mrs M: What do you call a purse like this that you can see through? Its a long word . . . transparent. If you can see through it, it's transparent.
Mrs M: Dinner children. Are you going to count yourselves?
Children: (In unison.) One, two, three . . . 27.

9.15   School assembly. The children move off into another classroom for assembly taken by the head. Mrs M uses the time to put materials out on the tables.

9.30   The children return and gather on the mat again. Mrs M spends a few minutes discussing the day of the week chart – day, month and weather – and then talks about the classroom clock.

9.38   Mrs M now sets up the mathematics work.
Mrs M: Table 1. You will continue what you were doing on

Friday. Sorting out a number on to sets. You will need pegs and boards.

Table 2. Show me your hands. Now table 2 are going to do something with their hands. You are going to use one hand to draw with and one hand to draw round. I want you to get a piece of paper and make sure your hand will fit on it. Don't spread your hand out too far; I don't want your span but the length of your hand. Put your hand on the paper and go round the fingers and thumb with a pencil. Then I want you to cut your hand out and all of you to put your hands side by side. Then find the longest hand and the shortest hand and put them all in order of their sizes. There are seven of you so there should be seven hands.

Table 3. Sequences. You know what to do. I want you to work with the white cards.

Table 4. Sorting into tens with unifix on the number track.

Table 5. Take aways. So you will need counting bricks.

9.43 Mrs M quickly hands out exercise books which have been marked and the children move to their tables and start work.

During the next 27 minutes Mrs M moves from table to table but with the most time on tables 1 and 2.

The mathematics scheme is based on Fletcher's approach. Table 1 are using coloured pegs to partition a set of twelve into equal sub-sets. Table 3 and table 5 are using work cards. The children of table 4 are working on the floor setting out unifix blocks in coloured sets of tens to make a hundred and putting small tiles with the cardinal numbers on in sequence.

10.05 *Mrs M:* I've found someone who hasn't started a card yet. (On table 2: Robert.) You have to do your mathematics and writing before dinner time or you will have to do it this afternoon.

10.14 Everyone had now moved to sit on the mat.

Table 4 is asked to explain what has been done on the number track and then the 'hands' of table 2 are examined. This provides a number of points for class discussion.

10.30 The children collect by the door, put on their coats and file out into the playground – except for Robert who is required by Mrs M to continue working because he has done so little.

Playtime

10.45 The children return and sit on the mat. First there is five minutes of flash card practice for the class in unison. The words are from the 'green books' in use in the classroom, e.g. are, engine, sun, into, magic, waiting, stations, sweet, far . . . Mrs M uses them for phonic practice as well as whole words.

Mrs M: What about this one. It's a little word but I'm not sure if you know it. (Holds up 'far'.)

Children: Far.

Mrs M: Oh good. Now, what is that sound? (She covers the 'f' with her fingers.)

Children: Ah!

Mrs M: If I chop off the 'fe' and put a 'je' what would it be? . . .

10.51 Mrs M had collected some pussy willow and horsechestnut buds over the weekend and these are used for class discussion. Words like 'sticky', 'shiny' and 'furry' are used.

11.02 Next comes the news time.

Sasha: We played a game of snakes and ladders . . . and I won. I got a hundred.

Christopher: My Grannie went to South Africa and brought me a T shirt. (He pulls up his pullover to reveal a T shirt covered in zebras.)

Joanna: Our telly broke down . . .

Each item provides opportunities for discussion.

11.20 Mrs M: My goodness. Look at the time. Right, we'll get started. Table 1: I want you to do the Yellow Book work cards. Use your writing books.

Table 2: Most of you have got three or four lines to finish to your Peru stories. I can't put them in the story book until you have quite finished.

Table 3: Some work cards to do with sounds. I'll come and see you.

Table 4: Now, you will need scissors and a gluepot. This is to be a sounds book. (She holds up a large green scrapbook with a letter written at the top of each page.) Yesterday I went through some old books and I found lots of pictures. Now you can cut them out, say the word to yourself . . . and stick them into the page that has the sound that starts the word. Decide where it goes and put them in tidily and leave room underneath for the name which I'll put in later when you tell me what to write.

Table 5: Some pirates, with pictures and sentences please. You will need pencils and crayons, all except table 4 – and you will need scissors. (She gives out some exercise books.) Get started straight away.

11.23 Everybody moves to the tables and work starts. Mrs M moves from table to table helping as necessary. During this period she hears two girls read – about three minutes each, but interrupted by other children with short requests. Children are encouraged to find their answers rather than ask.

Mrs M: You want to find the word 'house'. Why don't you look for it in the word book in the corner?

[Some details of the work at different tables:

Table 1. The work cards are linked to 'Through the Rainbow' e.g. < Find page 9: 1 What are the children playing with? 2 What have they made in the sand? 3 Draw a picture of them playing.>

Table 2. These children are writing their own stories about two children in Peru. Some words which may be useful have been written on a display board and they use their own alphabetical word books where Mrs M writes words on request.

Table 3. These children have work cards such as < Draw: Two little chicks saying cheep. Find 5 words with the ch sound.

Table 4. They are cutting out pictures and pasting them in the book. Some work on the table and others on the floor.

Table 5. The children here are copying the words and drawing pictures from work cards like: <Here is the blue pirate's knife.>]

11.50   Mrs M: Listen please everybody. It's nearly time to finish. Table 4: Please will you collect the pictures which haven't been used into a pile and put all the rubbish in the bin. Tables 1, 3 and 5: finish off the card you are on now. Table 2: Leave your things in the middle of the table and if you've not had time to finish you can carry on after dinner . . . Now. Those of you on cards. Put the card you are working on in the middle of the book and then I can mark them tonight and woe betide anyone who has not worked hard today, they'll get extra work tomorrow.

11.55   Everyone is now sitting on the mat. Mrs M holds up the green book made by Table 4 and asks the class whether each picture in turn is in the right place. They find a picture of a book on the 'd' page.

11.59   The people who are going home for dinner leave and then the others go through to wash their hands for dinner, dismissed in terms of 'people whose names begin with "m", "p"' etc.

Dinner time

1.15   The children come in and sit on the mat. The register is called as in the morning. Mrs M then asks some number questions based on Easter cards and children answer individually. This is followed by

Mrs M showing the class story book – about two children called Rairu and Marilia; the children read the captions which Mrs M has written on each page.

1.27   The major activity for the afternoon is to continue working on the Easter baskets and cards. For this, different groupings of children to those of the morning are made.

Mrs M: Who hasn't yet painted a basket? Just put your hand up. (Six people are chosen.) You six; you will need aprons and will work on that table. Paint the bottom and the inside different colours and don't let any of the box show through.

Which of you haven't yet finished your Easter card? (Three are identified.) Who would like to start their Easter card? (Three more are chosen.) Go on that table and I'll come and help you in a minute.

Now, let's have six who have finished their basket and their Easter card.

Bridget, John, Sasha, Joanna and Clare you will have to find your baskets and when you have them sit at that table.

Joanne, you get some glue out and then I'll show you what to do. It won't take long to get the insides put together.

Right, who hasn't done a basket yet? Gail, Alison, Wendy, Paul and Sally, you can get the handles done. You'll get half of the job done today, won't you.

Robert: I haven't started yet.

Mrs M: Oh no. You get your writing done instead ... Now, quickly. Everybody go to their tables and start.

1.35   Everyone is busy at the different activities. As the children painting their baskets finish, Mrs M announces that there is space and more children arrive. As the Easter activities are completed people move onto various play activities. At one stage two girls are dressing up, two boys are building a plastic railway, one boy is making a plastic camera, three boys are working with Lego, one boy is drawing another on the chalkboard with fascinating detail and one girl is playing a tune (?) on the chime bars. Mrs M hears four people read. Otherwise she moves from table to table helping here, answering questions there, and keeping an eye on Robert who is finishing off his morning work.

2.17   Mrs M: Listen. We have five more minutes. Please try to finish what you are doing. Be ready to pack away then.

2.22   Mrs M: Tidy up time. (The children quickly clear the tables.)

2.27   Everyone moves on to the mat. There are now 12 minutes of talking about what has been done. Mathematical ideas and vocabulary are developed.

Mrs M: Can you tell me how Phillip has painted his box?

Lee: He's done three. One in the corner, one in the middle and one in the other corner.

Mrs M: Yes. He's counted in sets of three. How many sets of three has he got?

Children: Two.

Mrs M: Two sets of three. And how many holes all together, Gail?

Gail: Six.

Mrs M: Yes. Two sets of three are . . .

Children: Six.

Mrs M: We could say three sets of two. There's a set of two, there's a set of two and there's a set of two. How many sets of two make six?

Gail: Two.

Mrs M: Two sets? Three sets of two make six.

2.40   Out to play.

Playtime

2.53   The children come in quickly and sit on the carpet for storytime. Mrs M reads a story called 'Witzenspitzel'.

3.09   The dinner money purses are returned and people are sent to collect their coats according to colours that they are wearing – pink, navy blue, yellow, red, brown, green. Simon is left at the end because he doesn't realize his jumper is navy blue.

3.14   Mrs M: Hands together and eyes closed.

Children: Hands together, softly so,
Little eyes shut tight.
Father, just before we go,
Hear our prayers tonight. Amen.

Mrs M: Good afternoon children.

Children: Good afternoon Mrs M.

3.15   The children leave.

4.20   Mrs M leaves, having marked the work done by the children today, prepared a display and made a few notes for tomorrow's work.

Notes on classroom organization

Pattern of the day

The different kinds of activity and the time spent on them on this day were:

Administration, tidying up	30 mins
Class discussions and storytime	109 mins

Mathematics group work	31 mins
Writing group work	35 mins
Creative work and play activities	52 mins
School assembly	15 mins
Playtimes	28 mins
Total	5 hours

Mrs M felt that this was a typical day, although the amount of time spent in class discussion varies according to what arises. Each of the three sessions of the day always begins with a discussion on the mat, but they do not always end, as this time, on the mat. The first morning session is for mathematics work, which consists of groups working through the Fletcher scheme, as on the observed day, for three or four sessions of each week. The other sessions involve enrichment activities from Fletcher, e.g. pictograms, work with sets. The second session of the day, after morning playtime, varies. About two days a week follow the pattern of the observed day, while about three days a week entail everyone engaged in a comprehension exercise, copy writing or phonic work, written on the chalkboard. Typically this lasts from about 11.00 to 11.40 and the children who finish the class exercise go on to do work cards. During these sessions Mrs M hears individual children read aloud while devoting a minimum of time to keeping everyone else busy. After the children have finished the allotted amount of work they are free to do either extra work cards or to choose a number or reading game from the shelf. They can play with this apparatus on their own or in groups and usually do so on the mat. In winter a radio singing programme, movement and dance, and a piano singing session are fitted in the week, while during the summer term there is PE once or twice a week outside.

Grouping of the children

For mathematics and writing the children are divided into five groups and sit at the five tables. These groups were established in September on the basis of achievement in mathematics in the reception class in the previous year. By and large they correlate with age and the children on tables 1 and 2 are those who will transfer to the junior school next year, while tables 3, 4 and 5 will join other children from the parallel class to form 'top class' and spend one more year in this school. Mrs M does not reckon to change children from group to group during the year.

Classroom rules

This term is one I used to describe the various guidelines, constraints and expectations which the teacher has adopted, and made clear to the children, in order to organize the day-by-day affairs of the class. Perhaps the most important guideline is that mornings are for work and afternoons for play. A specific amount of work in mathematics and writing is set each morning, and if this is not completed during the morning it has to be finished in the afternoon, so some of the creative or play activity is forfeit. Apart from this there are just a few simple rules related to tidiness etc. Aprons must be worn for messy work: painting, glueing etc. At the end of the afternoon the shelves, book corner, shop and pile of newspapers must be left tidy. Mrs M commented on this in our follow-up discussion:

> The children know that they have got to work in the morning if they want to play in the afternoon. They seem to accept it. I think children do. I think in some places there is too much freedom given them; children like a set of rules. They like to work within a framework. It gives them a feeling of security.

Organization of three Rs work

Mathematics
All four classes in the school use the Fletcher approach. Mrs M has a double page chart in her notebook which is a record of the progress made by her five groups through about twenty items of the Fletcher syllabus. The school has a large stock of work cards, which are the Fletcher work books copied on to card, and each teacher draws from this basic stock as necessary and in addition makes her own supplementary cards as she finds necessary. Mrs M found that the Fletcher scheme needs to be supplemented on the practical side. The work of her five groups on any one day is carefully arranged so that she can concentrate her attention on tables which are starting new work. On the day of the time study she spent most of the time with tables 1 and 2.

Reading
There are four different reading schemes in use in this class: Pirate, Ladybird, Through the Rainbow and Kathy and Mark. Mrs M has a double page chart in her notebook which is virtually a record and reading scheme for each child; she varies the scheme according to the competence and likely interests of the individual. Each child is heard to read aloud twice a week. The welfare assistant hears some of the more competent readers on one of these occasions. With the better readers, Mrs M groups them in pairs or trios and they read aloud in turn in the group. Once the children have some fluency she puts an emphasis on understanding and so asks the reader to talk about what has been read. The children take their reading books home at night. Apart from reading books there are many other occasions in the day for reading: work cards, flash cards, displays, charts etc.

Writing
Each child has a word book for collecting words that he or she cannot spell when writing; Mrs M expects this to be opened at the initial sound page

when a child brings it to her for a word. There are also picture dictionaries and word lists around the room, according to the topics under discussion. The stimulus for writing comes from many sources. The Peru stories which feature in the time study started from a Time and Tune radio programme. Assembly themes, events of the year, news of the weekend and things brought into class all provide starting points. Comprehension work cards are used extensively, and Mrs M keeps a record of which tables have worked through which cards.

Organization of materials

For each session of the morning there are work cards and other materials to arrange. Mrs M checks the paint pots, glue and pencils once a day. Each week she prepares about twenty flash cards linked to the reading schemes. Various jobs are allocated once a week: one person to change, one to remember the dinner numbers each day etc.

About once a month Mrs M reckons to check the supply of sticky-back paper, coloured tissues, drawing paper etc. and to change some of the books in the library. Wall displays stay up for about a month.

On most days Mrs M spends about half an hour before school and an hour afterwards in the classroom preparing work, marking, planning, keeping records and taking down and replacing displays. Rough plans for each day are written on a small note pad.

Each child has a drawer in a set of lockers. It contains writing book, number book, word book, reading book and from time to time a writing book on a specific topic, such as Bible stories, nature, people at work.

Records

Mrs M keeps these records: tick list of reading heard day by day; record of books each child has read; group record of stages in the mathematics scheme; group record of language comprehension cards tackled; record of class discussion topics; and wall displays through the year. At the end of each year she will make out a record sheet for each child for the information of the next teacher. This will give an indication of achievement in mathematics and reading and some indication of personal difficulties or emotional problems.

A day in Mrs W's classroom: a theory-seeking case study

General description

The school is in a well-to-do council estate five miles from the centre of

Nottingham and set in spacious grounds. It is a separate infant school with headteacher, seven class teachers and various ancillary staff. Across the playground is a junior school to which the children transfer in the September following their seventh birthday. The school was opened in 1963 and consists of six classrooms surrounding a hall, outside patio and staffroom. The seventh class uses an alcove off the hall. The construction is mainly brick and glass, is one storey and all on the same level. Mrs W's classroom is like this: there is a 'messy' corner, a home corner, a number corner and a quiet area; in between there are sets of tables for writing. At this time there are 30 children on roll, 19 girls and 11 boys, aged 5–6. Mrs W is the deputy head. She has been teaching for eight years and is 29 years old.

Time study

8.25   Mrs W arrives and checks on the different areas of her room.

8.50   Door opens. Groups of children come in during next five minutes, some with an adult, talk to Mrs W, take coats off, look at plants which have grown from some of the seeds planted last week and then sit on the carpet.

9.07   Mrs W checks the register and collects the dinner money.

9.15   Mrs W moves to a seat on the other side of the carpet, the children turn towards her and they then discuss the results of the seed planting. Gerbil food and budgie food have produced long green shoots like thick grass, but the tomato, apple and orange pips have produced nothing. A potato in the dark of a sealed box is examined; beans in jam jars have made some shoots, two onions have produced long roots and the water smells strongly.

9.26   Mrs W returns to her chair and the children swivel round again. She spends a couple of minutes revising work on the calendar, which is displayed on a stand.

9.29   Mrs W stands and in the next three minutes organizes the children's work for most of the morning.

    Mrs W: I'd like some help today to make *Our Book of . . .* (She holds up a scrapbook with *Our Book of Faces* written in large letters on the cover and points to the last word.)

    Children: . . . (various guesses) . . .

    Mrs W: It is. Good girl. You are clever. *Our Book of Faces.* Who's going to help me make this book of faces? (Many hands wave at her.) Andrew. Would you help me again? And Julie. And Simon. And Russell. We'll have those four people helping me to make my book of faces. What do we want to see in this book?

    Children: . . . faces . . .

    Mrs W: It can be a boy's face, a girl's face, a baby's face, a lady's face, a daddy's face, an old man's face, a grandma's face, a cat's face, any faces at all. There you are Andrew; there's the book. You four off you go. You start it and I'll come and help you soon. There are some books out on the table for you.

(Andrew, Julie, Simon and Russell move off the carpet to table D.)

Mrs W: Kevin brought us some new clay last week. To work with the clay you must roll your sleeves up as high as they will go and you must have an apron on, which must be fastened. Who would like to work in the clay? (Many hands go up.) Chelsea, Kirsty, Beverley and Tina may work in it first and when they have finished there will be some spaces, won't there? (These four children move to the clay table.) Apron on Chelsea. Sleeves rolled up as far as they will go.

I want to hear the boys read today. So Mark and Simon get your books out first and sit in the book corner . . . Michelle. Remember last week I was talking about the work book I was going to give to some of the very big children? Well, will you come to my desk; I've got one for you this morning. You can start yours off today. Mark and Simon. Just sit down until everybody else is busy. Now don't forget, everybody. You've got some number work to do. Best thing is not to leave it all till the afternoon. Plan your day and decide when you are going to do it. Right, everybody busy please.

9.32   The children move quickly. A rush for the home corner – but only the first four stay. Others move elsewhere. For the next forty-five minutes the children are busy individually or in groups:

Home corner: Lynn, Lorraine, Jo-anne, Sharon. Cooperative play partly influenced by a huge pair of giant's feet which have been previously painted and fixed to the wall which makes it look as though the giant is above the roof.

Faces cutting out table: Simon, Katy, Andrew, Russell. Mainly individual work sorting through magazines, cutting out faces and pasting these into the book; some interaction between children.

Clay: Beverley, Chelsea, Kirsty, Tina. Individual work on same table. Chelsea made a coiled pot, Kirsty a model of a footballer with rolled pieces laid flat on to card, Beverley made odd shapes with small pieces (I don't know what these were to her), Tina made patterns in a large flat piece.

Writing table A: Christina, Dawn, Bridget, Gina.

Writing table B: Peter, Karl, Annette, Deborah, Jane.

Writing table C: Julia, Michelle.

These children are either writing – about a dinosaur, about vegetables etc. – at various levels from tracing to work books, or are doing number work cards such as: You have 6 sweets and you eat 3. How many are left?

Reading corner: Mark, Simon.

Bricks: Michael, David, Stephen, Julian.

Mrs W spends this period in three activities: sitting in her chair hearing the boys read; sitting in her chair and responding to children who queue up to see her, for help with their writing or to show that their writing or number work is completed (this is then ticked and entered in her 'tick' book); moving round the groups to help here, encourage there, resolve a quarrel etc.

10.15   *Mrs W*:   In two minutes it will be biscuit time so finish what you are doing.

       Mrs W: Right Class 3. Put down what you are doing. You can go back and finish your model later on, or your piece of writing or your number work. Is the home corner tidy now? . . . Hang up your aprons. Wash your hands if they're dirty. Put your chairs under and make your place nice and tidy and then everybody ready for biscuits . . . Now, Simon, bring the biscuit box over to here. We won't start serving till everybody is ready . . . Right. All the girls with biscuit money come and line up please . . .

Mrs W uses the issue of biscuits as an opportunity for number work:

       Mrs W: Two halves. What do two halves make?

       Children: One.

       Mrs W: One penny. And she had another one as well so how much did she have?

       Children: Two.

       Mrs W: Two. That's right.

10.28   *Mrs W*:   Now Class 3. Listen. This is playtime. If you are going out to play put your coats on. You don't have to change your shoes, but you mustn't go on the grass. If you are staying in, what do you do? . . . You carry on with your work. And what do you do when the others come in from playtime?

       Children: Pack up.

       Mrs W: You start to pack up straight away because we have only a short time haven't we before service.

10.30   About eight children have left the classroom for the playground; the rest are busy. Mrs W goes to the staff room.

Playtime

10.50   Mrs W returns to the classroom and organizes the tidying up of the classroom. There is a great bustle in which everybody has a job to do.

Mrs W: Everybody packing up. You've had a long playtime this morning. Everybody packing up. Lorraine, go and help with the sand. Put them in the cupboard, Simon. Ssh. Don't want to see anybody standing about. I can see lots of jobs that everybody can help with . . . Hurry up. What's that string doing there? Throw that out . . . Lots of paper over here. Come on. Quickly. All this paper off the table. Come on, Michael, you're good at collecting rubbish . . .

10.58   The clearing up is completed within eight minutes and the children sit on the carpet for a brief discussion with their teacher. They then form two lines by the door.

11.02   The two lines file into the hall for service.

Service

11.25   The children return to the classroom and sit down on the carpet. Mrs W sits in her chair. After a quick revision of the months of the year Mrs W draws attention to the clay work, which is new to the classroom.

Mrs W: We have had four people very busy in the clay. Kirsty. Show us what you have made. (Kirsty shows her footballer and announces that it is a lady footballer.) . . . Now tell us all about this lady.

Kirsty: She has a necklace on . . . and a bracelet and a wig . . . When she was kicking the ball one of her diamonds came off –

Mrs W: Oh dear. Oh dear.

Kirsty: – and she couldn't find it and then she started crying.

This develops into a discussion about football and Mrs W recounts her visit to Twickenham of last Saturday. Everybody listens intently. Chelsea's coil pot is examined and then the faces book produced by Andrew, Karl, Russell and Julie.

11.55   The dinner children wash their hands, the others put their coats on, and within a couple of minutes the room is empty.

Dinner time

1.26   The door opens and children come in, take coats off and move on to the carpet. A mother comes and talks to Mrs W about the number work cards that her son is having difficulty with. Informal discussion is followed by the register.

1.34   It is quite foggy outside and Mrs W focuses attention on it.

Mrs W: I went out at dinner time in a car and I noticed that a lot of cars had got to put their lights on. Why's that? Why've they got to put their lights on in the middle of the day?

Children: It's because it's foggy.

Mrs W: It's because it's foggy. Yes it is foggy, isn't it. Look out of there. I can just see the trees the other side of the fence on the playground. Wonder if those will disappear into the fog soon? Have to keep our eye on them. Lorraine. You stand up and go and look out of that door. You can be our fog lady today. Tell me if you can see the trees, the little trees. Can you see them? The other side of the fence – two. Right, come back here now. What number is the big hand on the clock?

Lorraine: Eight.

Mrs W: It's on eight. When it gets up to the top, to twelve, I want you to look out of the window again and see if you can still see those two trees, and if you can't see them we'll know the fog has got thicker. (Pause.) What is fog?

The discussion turns to memories of last week's experiment with a cloud coming from a kettle of boiling water. Later a new experiment is set up with the plants which have grown from the hamster food. One is to be kept in the dark and another deprived of water. Then the afternoon activity period is started.

1.46   *Mrs W*: Now. Where's my friend Kirsty? How about writing that lovely story about the lady footballer? That funny story that made everybody laugh. Would you like to write it this afternoon for me?

I'll give you a piece of paper for it, instead of your book and when it's finished, if it's very nice, we shall put your footballer up on the wall, somehow, we shall try and make it stand up and we shall put the story beside it so everybody who comes into our room can read about that funny lady footballer –

Kirsty: Can I put my name?

Mrs W: Oh yes, put your name, we want to know whose work it is don't we. Do you remember that book that Andrew lent us last week . . . Desmond the Dinosaur and at the back of the book it said if anybody wanted to write a story about Desmond and send it off to the people who made the book then we could do so, couldn't we? Do you want to write one, then Lorraine? . . . Oh yes. Not the same story as we read – a different story about Desmond. Do you want to do one about Desmond, Annette?

Chelsea: Mrs W, can I make another thing in the clay?

Mrs W: Well I think you ought to do some other sort of work, Chelsea, and let somebody else have a go in the clay.

Everybody wanted to go in it this morning and you did have a turn and made something that is really nice. You children go away and think of your stories. Don't start writing till you've really thought of your story . . . Put your hand up if you would like to work in the clay. (About twenty hands go up.) Karl may. Gina may. I shan't choose anyone who stands up. You know you don't behave like that. Jane, I saw some work from you this morning. You may go in the clay. Yes, I said Karl. Make sure your sleeves are rolled up high Karl, won't you, because it's a bit messy. Ssh. I think we'll just have three in the clay this afternoon. Now the rest of you if you have not done your writing you know that it is the first thing you do because you won't have time if you leave it longer . . . If you have not started your writing yet go and get it out and get it started.

Child: Could we make a big book of the stories?

Mrs W: Yes. We could make a big book of them – couldn't we. David, I haven't seen yours. Off you go and get it out. You haven't done your number work? Good girl you go and do it then, and Dawn have you done yours? You have done all of yours haven't you. Good girl. What are you going to do now then? Yes of course you can. (To story children.) Have you thought of one? Well get your word books out ready then.

1.50 Everyone by now is busy. Mrs W sits down at writing table A to give the story writers some words. For the next thirty five minutes the pattern of work is:

Clay: Karl, Gina, Jane

Writing table A: Stephen, David, Bridget, Annette.

Writing table B: Peter, Christina, Simon, Michael, Kirsty, Chelsea, Michelle, Beverley.

Writing table C: Tina, Katy, Julie, Lynn, Jo-Anne.

Writing table D: Sharon, Julia, Lorraine, Andrew.

These children are writing about a variety of things and some are doing number work.

Sand tray: Dawn, Deborah (after a few minutes).

Mrs W spends part of the time in her chair giving words and recording when children have completed a piece of work, and part at the various tables helping the children. From about 2.15 on she calls to various children where there is a gap in her tick book – showing that the child has not completed today's work. Several boys move to the bricks, also Kirsty.

	Mrs W:	(To Simon) You have only written one word this afternoon – I'm not very pleased with you.
2.21	*Mrs W:*	Class 3. You have five minutes left before playtime to finish your work.
2.26	*Mrs W:*	Chelsea, Mark and Tina. It is now playtime. You must finish your work before you go out. If the rest of you want to go out put your coats on.

2.30   Mrs W leaves the classroom for her afternoon break.

Playtime

2.50   Mrs W returns. All the children seem to be back.

Mrs W: Stop what you are doing, please Class 3. Simon I want your book put on my desk please. Where's Tina? Has she gone out? Well there will be trouble for Tina. Put all your books away. Peter! Don't make a noise. Ssh. Everybody on to the mat, quickly. Ssh . . . Tina. I am not pleased with you. You had better bring me your writing and your number work that you should have done. Everybody sitting down, quickly . . .

2.55   Tidying up for the end of the day now begins.

Mrs W: Now nobody has painted this afternoon so – is it Julia and Gina who do the paint corner? No, Sharon and Gina, will you put the clay away for me instead. Roll your sleeves up and put an apron on. Roll the clay into balls and put it back in the bucket. Everybody else should know their job . . . If you have finished your job quickly what do you do? You don't sit down, Lorraine. You help somebody else, right. Everybody packing up please.

3.00   By this time the children are sitting on the mat again, having cleared up the room. Mrs W, from her chair, invites people to show anything which they have brought from home. Someone shows a Rupert book, Stephen some keys on a ring, Deborah a finger ring. Michelle has two socks which her father has made into animal faces and which she wears on her hands. Mrs W picks up the idea of this and suggests that anyone who wants to make one like this should bring an old sock; when Mrs R comes she may help them with the sewing. Lorraine has some shapes of paper carefully carried in a brown paper bag. Jo-Anne has her father's car keys; she says he has gone on the bus to save petrol. Annette has a wooden spoon with two faces on it – one happy and one sad. Again Mrs W develops this: 'Tomorrow we will help you dress it.'

3.13   Mrs W tells the story of the Old Man and the Turnip Seed and acts it out with some of the children. Obviously a tremendous favourite.

3.24   Coats on and goodbye. Mrs W stays in school for a further hour, preparing teaching materials and displays.

Notes on classroom organization

Pattern of the day

The different activities and time spent on them on this particular day were:

Informal discussions, administration, packing up etc.	75 min
Class discussion led by Mrs W and storytime	85 min
Individual group activities	80 min
Playtime or continuation of individual and group activities	40 min
School service in the hall	25 min
Total	5 hr 5 min

From day to day, the time spent on teacher-led class discussion varies. On this particular day it was longer than usual, as Mrs W explained in our follow-up discussion.

> The class discussion varies a lot. Some days we go straight into individual work; there might be nothing that they wanted to discuss; they might not bring anything in; there might be nothing in the room that immediately attracted their attention like the growing things. They might just come in and sit down and look at me ready for the register. On this day I drew attention to the clay because it was new in the room, but if I'm not setting up anything special for that day, we just go straight into our work. Especially in the afternoon this happens. It's not often that we have a discussion at the beginning of the afternoon.

The position of school assembly in the day had been changed a few weeks earlier from 9.15 to 11.00. Mrs W prefers the new arrangement because if an idea for some work arises first thing in the morning the children can go straight into it without the interruption of school service; otherwise some of the children, especially the younger ones, may lose interest.

Mrs W has no definite name for the periods of general activity when children are working individually or in groups. She tends to call it 'work time'. In the week there are some minor variations in this pattern – for physical education in the hall, for singing lessons with a pianist and very occasionally for television programmes – but in general this pattern is followed by Mrs W throughout the year. The use of playtime in this classroom is particularly interesting because for many children it extends the time they can spend working at individual or group activities from an average of just over one and a half hours per day, to about two hours. As indicated in the time study, Mrs W allows most of the children to decide whether or not they want to go outside during playtime, but if they haven't finished their writing or number work in the afternoon activity period she insists on it being completed then. At this time of the year (February) most of the children choose to stay in the classroom and they work sensibly without supervision. One teacher is on duty during each playtime and keeps a roving eye on the classrooms, but it is unusual for there to be trouble. I asked Mrs W about this.

MB: Do you ever get any difficulties with children in the classroom on their own?

Mrs W: Sometimes someone will abuse it. I repeat every time I go out of the room the same points. 'Are you staying in? If you are staying in what are you going to do? And they all say: 'Work.' And I say, 'Yes. It's a *work* time. If you want to have a play-time you go outside'. It has to be reinforced all the time . . . I think it is better having an option. Some children do need a time when they rush about and shout: some go out every time there is a break, but some just never want to.

Classroom rules

Underpinning the whole organization of the classroom are the rules governing the children's activities. Mrs W doesn't really like the term 'rule' but some term is needed to describe the various guidelines, constraints and expectations which the teacher makes overt to the children. They are not, of course, written down anywhere, but are part of the understanding between teacher and class. The transcripts in the time study show the way in which Mrs W frequently reminds the children of what she expects of them.

This is my list of Mrs W's classroom rules.

1 Everyone must do at least one piece of writing per day. According to the age of the child the nature of the writing varies. For the very youngest it may be no more than a scribble picture in their writing book and Mrs W writing a word like 'cat' or 'my house' at his or her suggestion underneath.
2 Everyone must do some number work each day. For those who can read work cards the expectation is three of these cards per day. For the others it may be individual or group work of a counting kind.
3 When the writing or number work is complete for the day, it must be taken to Mrs W. (She responds and puts a mark in her 'tick book'.)
4 Everyone must read aloud to Mrs W at least once every two days.
5 Certain of the resources of the room have a limit fixed for the number of children who may work there at one time: home corner 4, bricks 4, sand 2, painting easels 4.
6 When any piece of work is complete the materials must be cleared away before any new activity is started.
7 Aprons must be worn and sleeves rolled up by children doing painting, water or clay work.
8 Coats must be hung on pegs and not dropped on the floor.
9 Hands must be washed before school dinner.

After we had identified these rules, Mrs W qualified them.

But the rules aren't all that strict. I am thinking of Michelle. Yesterday she decided she would write first of all; she is doing *The Tale of the*

Turnip. It has taken her about three weeks. She does a little bit of writing every day on the same story. I think it is quite an achievement for a five-year-old to keep the interest going. Yesterday she didn't do any number work at all and when I was checking through my tick book at quarter past two, as I normally do, I said 'Who has not done any number work yet? Michelle stood up and looked very upset about it, but I wasn't at all cross with her because she hadn't wasted a minute of the day; she'd written all day long. I don't demand number work always – it depends upon the individual child.

Organization of three Rs work

These notes are limited to organizational aspects of three Rs work and do not include details of reading scheme or number curriculum.

Number work

Mrs W explained how number work is organized in terms of three stages of the development of reading/writing skills.

> Mrs W: Some of the children are not recording any number yet because they can hardly control a pencil – so it's pointless setting them on recording . . . They can't count on their own, so we just talk and count beads and such like. We count milk bottles and the straws put in the bottles. I ask 'How many coats are hanging up?' and other questions like this. Those who can copy under my writing, but can't yet copy from a card or book – I write a number problem in their books – I might write just one piece of work, or sometimes as many as five – it depends so much on the individual child. When they have the ability to copy from a card I expect them to do three number cards per day.
>
> MB: I noticed how often counting exercises were coming up in the day.
>
> Mrs W: Yes. All the time. You learn to talk with a number vocabulary. The possibilities are endless. Taking off a child's coat you can bring number in: 'How many buttons have you undone now? One sleeve is empty; two sleeves are empty. Is your coat bigger than Mary's?'

Reading

Mrs W hears the boys read aloud individually on one day and the girls on the next. Her system is to call them to her one by one and to work steadily through her list; in consequence there is not the pressure met in other classrooms of the children asking if they may read to her.

MB: Roughly how long do the children have each to read to you?

Mrs W: It varies. About two or three minutes. It depends upon the individual child. I've got some children who have no idea about reading yet. They don't know that you start at the front of a book and that you read from left to right and that one word is a group of letters . . . Other people like Michelle are reading almost fluently.

MB: How does the card system work – the cards they keep in their reading book?

Mrs W: I put on the card the title of the book and the page that they have reached. When they have become fairly competent – not fluent but when they know what it is all about and they are making rapid progress you can't really hear them as often as you would like and as often as they would like, so I allow the mums and dads to mark off three pages on the card – I talk to them first about testing the children on the words – in terms of questions like 'What does that word say? Show me "made". Show me "John".'

MB: What do you put on the card?

Mrs W: I put the page that they have just finished on the card and a tick beside it. That's not the only reading that we do – there is more than just reading from their reading books. There are number cards to read, they read their writing back to me, if they can, and we make group books which they read – for example, we made a book recording what we had found out about vegetables. I've written it in large writing and they can take it into the book corner and read it.

Writing

Throughout the school four stages in the development of writing are recognized:

1 The child traces on top of words which the teacher has written in response to the child's description of a picture which the child has drawn in his or her writing book.
2 Similar, but the child copies the teacher's writing underneath the words.
3 The child dictates a few words which the teacher writes in the child's 'sentence book' and the child then copies these into his or her writing book.
4 The child has an alphabet book which she or he opens at the appropriate page and brings to the teacher for her to write in the word she or he needs in constructing his or her own sentences. (At this time – February – two children in this class of 5–6-year-olds were on alphabet books.)

I asked about the children making *Our Book of Faces*.

These children need a lot of help with hand coordination; they can't use a pencil very well, or scissors, so this was an activity specially for that . . . I think some of the children have never handled scissors before they come to school. It also brings in quite a lot of discussion. We've made all sorts of books like 'Things in our kitchen' and 'Things we can eat' which use the same skills.

Organization of materials

Mrs W likes to think of her classroom as a workshop and she stressed the importance of keeping the tools for learning tidy and in good repair. Early every morning she checks her room:

Painting area:	Is there sufficient paint? (Paint is normally made up once a week.) Is it in working order? Is there enough paper?
Collage table:	Is there sufficient collage paper? Are the materials ready for use? (Usually replenished once a week; tray of materials cut into small pieces of different sizes, a tray of lace, a tray of wool, a tray of assortments – packaging paper, straws, tissue, wire . . .) Is the glue sufficient and in working order? (Polycell, mixed up in quantity from time to time.)
Boxwork table:	Check the glue.
Writing tables:	Are the pencils sharp?

At the end of each morning and afternoon there is a quick tidying up session. Each child has a particular job and these are allocated at the beginning of each half term. For example:

- two children wash paint brushes and wipe out the pots;
- two children sweep up sand from the floor;
- four children tidy the home corner;
- two children pick up pencils and crayons from the floor etc.

Particular care is taken over the clay, since this can go hard and be unusable very easily. After use it is rolled into balls, thumbs are pushed in to make a simple 'thumb pot', water is put in the depression and the 'pots' are then stood in the clay bucket with a moist cloth over the top.

From time to time other maintenance tasks are necessary. For example:

Sand tray:	Dry sand needs to be sifted regularly to remove unwanted objects. If the sand is being used wet it needs to be cleaned off the sand apparatus.
Water tray:	(Either sand or water are regularly available in this classroom, but not both, because together they produce

	a mess on the floor which is difficult to clear up.) The water is changed as soon as it looks dirty.
Boxwork:	Unsuitable cartons need to be thrown away.
Home corner:	The tea sets need washing and broken items are thrown away. Dressing up clothes, tablecloths and curtains need washing and ironing.
Book corner:	These books are changed once every two weeks from the classroom book store cupboard. (The store cupboard books are changed once every six months. About 70 books are on display in the classroom at any one time and there are perhaps 500 books in the store cupboard.)
Bricks:	These need sorting to remove odd items like dirty handkerchiefs.
Display shelves:	Dusting.
Drapes used for display:	These need washing and ironing, which is done by the cleaning staff.

At the end of each half-term the walls are completely stripped of displays so that the cleaners can clean them thoroughly. Dressmakers' pins and 'Blutak' are used to hold up displays – not drawing pins.

Each child has a deep plastic tray with his or her name on the front and kept in one of two locker units. The contents include:

1 Current writing book. (Made by Mrs W, or by a parent-helper, with a thin card cover and 10 sheets folded to make 40 pages. Earlier in the year Mrs W makes these of six sheets: the point is to achieve a balance between keeping a record of day-to-day achievement and the pleasure of starting a new book. The youngest children do a drawing on one page and copy writing on the opposite page; as they become more competent and their writing becomes smaller they put a drawing at the top of the page and write underneath; later they may dispense with drawings and write from page to page.)
2 Current number book (similar to the writing book).
3 Word book (either 'sentence' or 'alphabet': see above).
4 Reading book.
5 'Work book'. These are for the older children where from time to time they respond to enquiry work cards like 'What is a man called who sells fish?' and 'Tell me four things that are red'.
6 'Treasures', i.e. small personal possessions.

Mrs W has a filing box with a compartment for each child and completed writing books and number books are stored there.

Records

Mrs W keeps a 'tick book' as a check that the children are regularly engaging in written work, number work and reading aloud. There is a list of the children down the left-hand margin of the page and for each day two vertical columns – in one she puts the page that the child has finished reading, and in the second column an N for the completion of number work and a W for the writing. She doesn't keep this record every day, but about three times a week. She added that if the class were of older infants she would keep the record every day.

No record is kept of individual work at other activities. At the back of the tick book Mrs W keeps a note of the books which the children have read, and also a brief record of stories read to them, discussions held and poems and songs learned.

Each half-term Mrs W makes notes on each child's emotional and social development and puts in the record scrapbook a sample of her or his written work and number work. She also records in diary form the major events of the half-term: the interests that have arisen, how they developed and what they led to.

A day in Mr A's classroom: a theory-seeking case study

General description

The school is in a social priority area on the outskirts of a city in the East Midlands. It is a junior school with ten classes, three of which are located in a nearby annex. Mr A's classroom is in the main building, which was erected about seventy years ago. It is one of several classrooms opening into a central hall, which is used for assembly and for individual study in a carpeted library area. Physical education lessons and school dinners are taken in a separate building. The area of the classroom is 56 square metres. There are 36 children in the class: they are mixed third and fourth years; that is, aged 9–11. Mr A is 44. He originally trained and worked as a librarian. He has now been teaching for 15 years and is deputy head of the school.

Time study

8.25 Mr A arrives at school. Coffee in staff room. Prepares classroom.
8.57 Boy comes in to discuss personal difficulty.
9.00 School bell rings. Children come in and sit down; some talk to Mr A. By the time the register is called nearly everyone, without being told to, has a reading book out.
9.03 *Mr A:*   When you're ready we'll have the register. Numbers please, David.

David:	One sir.
Mr A:	Kevin not here, oh!
Paul:	Three sir.
Philip:	Four sir.
. . .	(Kevin arrives during the roll call.)
Mr A:	You've made it Kevin. My word you look desperate. Sit down, tell me about it when you've recovered.

Roll call takes just 60 seconds and is followed by the school dinner list which takes 100 seconds to resolve. Kevin comes to Mr A's desk.

9.06	*Mr A*:	Right, Kevin. What happened then?
	Kevin:	I've got an alarm clock and my mum set it for quarter to nine.
	Mr A:	Ah! Quarter to nine instead of what?
	Kevin:	Half-past eight.
	Mr A:	Is that when you set it for? Oh, I should make it quarter past eight if I were you Kev.

During the next few minutes, while most people are reading, arrangements are made for recording the weather today and for housing a guinea pig.

9.10	School bell rings.	
	Mr A:	Would you stand quietly please. We have Mr R this morning (for assembly) and after that it's normal reading.

The children make a line by the door, of their own accord, and, at a signal from Mr A, file out into the hall.

9.12 Classroom empty except for Mr A who prepares teaching material. He joins the assembly at 9.32 for the notices.

9.36 The children return, collect their reading books and move to the appropriate classroom for their reading groups. Those of Mr A's reading group who come from other classes now arrive. There are 20 in his reading group. They begin reading of their own accord, while Mr A talks to individuals. Stephen says that he isn't enjoying *Shane*.

Mr A:	Oh, what a tragedy. I'll tell you what. Give it two more days. You've only read one chapter. It's a bit slow in action at the beginning until the baddie comes into town. Give it another couple of days and then we'll discuss it again, Stephen. It's really not bad.

9.42 Most people are reading silently but a few are chattering. In a quiet voice:

Mr A:	Can I remind you that this is a reading group. Some of you seem to have forgotten.

The chattering ceases immediately. During the next 20 minutes Mr

A hears six children read and discusses their reading with them individually.

10.04   School bell rings to mark the end of the reading groups. The children belonging to other classes leave and those who have been reading elsewhere return to this class.

10.06   Mr A is now standing by the blackboard and for the next half-hour he leads the class in discussion linked to investigations which are in progress in the classroom at present: weather studies, Victorian times and the murderess Mary Ann Cotton, a book on British coins, old photographs of Nottingham. Then Mr A draws attention to today's newspaper and the execution in the United States of Gary Gilmore. Discussion of the rights and wrongs of capital punishment follows: only six people put their hands up in support of the execution of murderers as an alternative to long imprisonment.

10.40   School bell rings for playtime. Everyone goes out. Mr A has coffee in the staffroom.

Playtime

10.55   School bell. Children come in and sit down.

Mr A: Will you take out from your desks your Beta Mathematics books . . . carry on from where you were.

Books 1, 2, 3, and 4 of the Beta Mathematics series and of the More Practice series are in use according to the ability of the individual child. Mathematics work is done at four levels on one topic at a time – at present the topic is graphs. Each child belongs to a mathematics group, which defines her or his level of work, and the assigned work is set out on an 'assignment card' which is pinned to the side of the blackboard. This card gives the mathematics work for the whole class for a period of several days:

> MATHS ASSIGNMENTS
> Beta Mathematics
>   Group 1 Beta 4 pages 8, 9, 10, 11, 12, 24, 25
>   Group 2 Beta 3 pages 25, 26, 27, 30, 31, 48, 51
>   Group 3 Beta 3 pages 6, 7, 21, 24, 25; Beta 2 pages 53, 54, 70
>   Group 4 Beta 1 pages 46, 47, 72, 73, 74
> More Practice
>   Group 1 Book 4 pages 15, 18, 19, 30
>   Group 2 Book 3 pages 16, 17, 22, 23
>   Group 3 Book 2 pages 6, 22, 23, 42, 43

The children stay in their class places so that each table has a variety of work in progress. Mr A sits at his desk for about half an hour and about twenty children come to him for help or to have their work marked. For the rest of the period he moves around the room from table to table, giving individual assistance. Only once during this hour does he interrupt the class to draw their attention to a particularly well drawn block graph:

Mr A: Could you just give me your attention for a second. I hope that when we get some more graphs from the group doing them they come out as nice as this one. It is beautifully done. He's not used too many colours – only two and so it doesn't look like a rainbow, you can concentrate on what it tells you. It's beautifully filled in; he's used a ruler, no lines overdrawn. It's got all the information in.

11.55   At the end of the morning careful instructions are given:

Mr A: (To one child) . . . hardly any mistakes at all. Well done. I don't think I should start another one now love, 'cause its five minutes to the end of the lesson. (To everyone, voice just slightly louder, but projected across the room, and spoken slowly.) Will you stop now, the one you are doing, and Andrew, will you check whether anyone is in the hall and we'll have them in the classroom. It's just possible, let's check, that there might be someone in the playground . . . Will you now close your book, carefully put it away in your box – in that neat, tidy box you have under your table top . . . (the bell rings). Stand up behind your chair now. If you're going for school dinner, line up now . . . Remember what I said about the line, you've forgotten.

The school dinner people file out and then the others leave. Mr A locks the classroom door. He has a quick lunch and then takes part in a staff meeting.

Dinner time

1.15   School bell rings. The children come in, mostly sit down and chat quietly.

1.19   Mr A: Sit down everyone, without exception. And when you're ready, not before, we'll have the register. Just one table not quite ready – almost – yes, I think we can start, well done. David.

David: One sir.
Kevin: Two sir.
Paul: Three sir . . .

1.20   Mr A: First of all stand up the boys and girls who are going to go cooking this afternoon. Six of you . . . You may go to your cooking then . . . Now the rest of you can read your county library books.

A selection of library books is available. Mr A moves around the room discussing the books with individuals and answering questions.

Mr A: Gosh, it's taken you a long time to finish that one Paul. How long have you had that now? Let's look at the date . . . Which one is that Shirley? I've forgotten which one you're reading. Oh, *The Case of the Silver Egg.* Tell me about it at the end because it's not one that I know.

1.44 *Mr A:* Right. Very quietly will you put the county library books away. Listen carefully to what your group is doing before play. Group 2, I would like you to carry on with the *Do You Know* books. Hands up group 2, there may be a few short this afternoon because of the cooking. Fine. Group 4, would you go on with the dictionary work please – the Red Dictionary . . . Group 3, the Victorian topic and poems. Group 1. Somebody from Group 1, Louisa, can you very carefully wheel in the tape recorder cabinet. I'll show you where it is . . .

David: Mr A. Can I go in the 'all

Mr A: Yes David. You may work in there.

Jacqueline: Mr A, please may I finish off my story?

Mr A: No. I'd rather you did this topic work please Jacqueline.

Everyone is soon busy at various tasks. Mr A circulates round the room helping and discussing with individuals. He organizes the poems group to make recordings of their chosen poems and Chris learns how to use the machine. This group is standing around the tape recorder and is working together; the other groups are working individually and are sitting at their class places so that each table has a variety of activities in progress.

The Red Dictionary people are using Black's *Writing Dictionary* with its associated quiz book, entitled *Find the Right Word.* Examples of the questions are:

page 7: The words you have to find on this page all come from the b section. The first word is near the beginning.

(a) Where does a *badger* live?

(b) Where do you place *bails*?

(c) *Ballet* is a special kind of . . .

(d) Another word for a *bandit* is a . . .

The *Do You Know* group are using Black's *Children's Encyclopaedia* and the associated quiz books. Examples of the questions are:

Book 12 (linked to Volume 12 of the encyclopaedia, Toronto–Zuyder Zee) page 8 ANIMAL

1 What kind of animals are vertebrates?

2 Where would you look for a field vole?

3 Where do walruses live?

4 What sound do walruses make?

The Victorian topic develops from work cards associated with readings and books. Four examples show the way in which Mr A pitches the work cards at different levels.

(yellow card)

Jesse James the Outlaw

Read the book first.

Answer with sentences.

1 Where did Jesse James live? (page 3)

2 What was his brother's name (page 3)

3 What happened when he was older? (page 4)

4 What did Jesse do? (page 5)

5 What happened after the war? (page 6)

(orange card)

Victorian Clothing

Read the back of the card.

1 When did Queen Victoria reign?

2 Name three ways in which life changed at this time.

3 What did men usually have on their heads? What else?

4 What is a crinoline?

5 Why is the lady in the picture crying?

6 What year is it in the picture?

(green card)

Use *Wash and Brush Up* (Eleanor Allen, A & C Black, 1976)

1 When Victoria became Queen how many bathrooms were there in Buckingham Palace? (page 30)

2 In old times, how did they get hot water to the bath? (page 30)

3 What is w.c. short for? (page 16)

4 What job did 'night soil' men do? (page 15)

5 Did Victorians use make up? (page 39)

6 How did girls make their hair shine? (page 43)

7 Where did they get false teeth after the battle of Waterloo? (page 48)

8 What was a mangle used for? (page 59)

(red card)

Use *Children's Britannica* (available in the School Library)

Find VICTORIA CROSS

1 When was the Victoria Cross first awarded?

2 What does it look like and what colour is the ribbon?

3 Is there any money for those who win it?

4 Who was the first winner?

     5 Roughly how many have been awarded?

     6 Write the story of one of the winners.

2.24   Anita asks Mr A to mark her quiz work. This is the last marking in this period. He sits next to her.

> Mr A: 'A beam is a thick heavy bar of wood.' Yes. 'Bisect – cut into two parts.' 'Bulldozer – a powerful machine.' You've got on very well with these. (He reads through a long list of answers and ticks each one) . . . 'Brass is a yellow coloured metal' . . . 'Bound is a leap called tied up.' Ah. It's two words 'bound', isn't it. It means to leap, which also means to . . .?
>
> Anita: To tie.
>
> Mr A: Yes, 'bound' means 'tied up' or it means 'leap'. Do you know what 'leap' means?
>
> Anita: Like 'jumping' isn't it?
>
> Mr A: Yes, exactly. It does. It means jump. So 'bound' means 'jump' as well. Well that's very good. You really have done some smashing work today, Anita, I'm going to give you another team point.
> Can we stop for a minute, please. I think after Chris has taken all this trouble to record some work on here I think we might well listen to what he has been catching. Shut the door, Ian. Quiet please then . . . and we'll listen.
> Everyone listens to the recordings, which last about two minutes. The limerick about 'The Young Lady from Ryde' causes some amusement.
>
> Mr A: That it Chris? Well, congratulations on some excellent recordings. You've got yourself a job there; but I expect we'd better have a deputy in case Chris gets tired of it. Very well done. I thought that one by Spike Milligan was well done and well chosen. It needs slowing down I think and also it's worth getting some instruments, with all those bongs and pings in the poem it would go very well.

2.30   The school bell rings.

> Mr A: Er. I'm going to collect the dictionary books, so Shaun, can I trust you to collect those up. There are two boys outside, in the library, Shaun . . . Once your desk is tidy, and that means there is nothing on it, you may go out.

Everyone leaves for afternoon playtime. Philip offers Mr A one of the cakes he has made. Mr A goes to the staffroom.

Playtime

2.50   The children return shortly after the bell has rung and they all sit down in their places. Mr A looks round to make sure everyone is in, and then:

Mr A: Ready. I'm going to put group 1 on to science work. Just a reminder that you put the results, or any working, in your science books. The cards are there and reasonably tidy. Andrew will be tidying them towards the end of the afternoon. I'll tell you the other groups in a moment when Paul has finished his conversation with Louisa. Are you quite ready, Paul? Group 3, I want you to try a music card, which we have over here. Not many of you have done them up to now and so I want you to start a new book for them. So would you collect one and collect a card. (He holds up a pile of school-made work books.) Put your name inside. Group 2, I want you to collect the map books, which are on the top shelf, and to carry on with them. I think you're on about the third section. And finally that leaves group 4 – poems.

2.53   Everyone starts work. Some of the science group work in a dark room off the hall with a torch. Others are working with magnets or batteries and bulbs. Louisa is puzzled by finding that when three bulbs are wired in a line only two of them light up. She tries various ways of making the third one light up and eventually succeeds.

The people working on maps are using Phillip's *Elementary Atlas* and Prater's *Look at Your Atlas*, which asks questions like:

Use your Atlas to find the names of the seas. Turn to your map of Europe.

1 Between Italy and Yugoslavia
2 To the north of Poland.

The new music work cards have been devised by Mr A. Some are practical and the others based on books. For example:

Choose three chime bars, B, A, G, from the music table. Next, choose a short poem from the poem cards. Try to make a tune, using these three notes, to fit the poem. Write the poem in your music book and write the notes under the words so that you will not forget it. (If you can write music write it on music paper.)

Use the book *The Orchestra* to answer these questions

1 What are the four families of musical instruments (page 14).
2 Name the three members of the string family (pages 23, 24, 25, 26).
3 Name six members of the woodwind family (pages 29, 35).
4 List four members of the brass family (page 36).
5 Draw, or trace, one instrument from each family.

As before Mr A moves round the room talking to individuals and discussing their work.

3.27   *Mr A:*   You have about five minutes before we pack up.

3.33   *Mr A:*   I now want the boys and girls who have been using musical instruments to do two things. First, put down any beater that they are using; second, put the music card back on the music table – they're very untidy at the moment – incidentally, I want that tidying up; and third, take the musical instrument back to the music room and if the music room is in a mess when I look at it after school, we shall be having a little discussion about it tomorrow, so make sure it's nice and tidy. Er, scientists. All the scientific equipment neatly away in its boxes . . . all the equipment away please Louisa . . . right, come on, quickly, two minutes . . . I think with the exception of Kerry, who is doing a little job, the rest of us can be seated. Stand up spelling group 2. As you're having a test tomorrow, I thought we might have a little reminder. How about the word 'daughter', Philip? That's all right, you may sit down. Brian, how about 'digging'? That's excellent. 'Dangerous', Andrew?

Andrew: D A N G E R O E S

Mr A: I should have another think about that one Andrew. I don't think you have been learning them over the weekend as I asked. You spell 'dairy' for us, Jackie. Yes. What is a dairy. Jackie? . . . Thank you. The rest of you sit down. The test will be tomorrow, so be ready for it.

Without further comment Mr A moves across the classroom, opens Ted Hughes's *The Iron Man* and begins to read.

Mr A: Slowly he covered the distance, getting smaller and smaller as he went. At last he landed, a ragged black shape, sprawled across the Sun; everybody watched and now they saw the Monster begin to glow, blue at first, then red, then orange, finally its shape was invisible, the same blazing white as the Sun itself, the Monster was white hot on the Sun . . .

the Dragon was weeping. If the Iron Man got onto his furnace again, it would mean that he, the Monster, would have to take another roasting in the Sun and he couldn't stand another. 'Enough, enough,' he roared. 'Oh no,' replied the Iron Man. 'I feel like going on. We've only had two each.'

3.45   (The school bell rings.)

I'll finish that off tomorrow. Very quietly put up your chair. Two things to remember for tomorrow. Please can we have some more comics and sometime tomorrow we will have the spelling test that you have been preparing

for, so no doubt you will do a bit of extra practice
tonight. Thank you. Good afternoon everybody.
(Children slowly leave.)

4.00   Mr A looks after the school badminton club in the hall.
4.30   Leaves school.

Notes on classroom organization

Patterns of the day

The different kinds of activity and the time spent on them on this day were:

Administration (with quiet reading)	15 min
Class discussion and story-time	45 min
Mathematics group work	65 min
Reading	53 min
Group work – various subjects	91 min
School assembly	26 min
Playtimes	35 min
Total	5 hr 30 min

Most days are similar, but might include craft or a physical education session, a swimming lesson or a class lesson on a particular subject. Mr A arranges the work of the class on a day-by-day basis according to the needs and mood of the class.

Groupings of the children

The children are seated six to a table according to decisions made by them at the beginning of the year. If individuals wish to change their places this is negotiated with Mr A. They stay in these places for all subjects, unless the particular work necessitates being elsewhere, or unless they have Mr A's permission to work in the hall. They are relatively free to move around the classroom, without asking permission, to consult books, collect paper, sharpen pencils etc.

Apart from this self-chosen grouping, which determines location in the classroom, four groupings reflect the children's level of attainment in different parts of the curriculum. For general work, including writing, topic, poetry and various activities in science, history, geography and music, there are four groups based on reading ability. There are also 11 groups based on reading ability across the whole school and which serve to divide the children for the reading sessions held for half an hour each morning. In mathematics there are four groups based on mathematical ability. There are also three groups for spelling.

Mr A and the children use, without confusion, numbers for all these groupings, as well as individual numbers for the register. Class social grouping is not necessarily linked to academic grouping.

Reading
Mr A puts great emphasis on reading, as does the whole school. For half an hour each morning the 10 classes of the school are regrouped according to reading ability and engage in silent reading and reading aloud in turn to their group teacher. Mr A has a further silent reading period in the afternoon for his own class and, as in the morning, he hears the children read aloud in turn and he discusses their story books with them individually. When a book is finished he asks for a short piece of writing about it. He classifies the books borrowed from the county library into three classes, designated by coloured cards slipped into the library 'book pocket', in order to facilitate selection by the children and to minimize the frustration which can be felt by selecting a book which is too hard to read. On a quick count there are over 400 books readily available to the children. The major areas are:

Encyclopaedias	12
Dictionaries	34
Atlases	9
English	63
Handwriting	24
Mathematics	45
Topics	56
Poetry	30
Geography	9
History	18
Science	25
Stories	89

Other books are stored in the children's work trays, and outside the classroom, in the hall, is the school library with many more volumes. Mr A makes a considerable use of work cards to direct study in various areas of the curriculum and sees this as an important part of the reading experience of the children.

Topics
Topics normally run for half a term in Mr A's classroom and, among other interests, he reckons each year to include at least one local environment topic, something scientific, something geographic and something historical. He decides the areas of study. During each holiday he spends a day or two in selecting thirty to forty books from the county library project collection, sorts them into three different levels of reading difficulty and writes appropriate work cards. He puts emphasis on children learning the skills of enquiry and he gives the class lessons in this as well as plenty of practice through work cards linked to the topic.

Other aspects of language
Regular spelling activities, comprehension exercises, 'bread and butter' lessons on punctuation, listening to stories and poetry – reading it quietly, aloud and discussing poems – all feature in the work of the week, in addition to regular writing coming from the topic and from other activities.

Mathematics
The four groupings usually work on the same aspect of mathematics but at different levels. At the time of the study, seven children were on Beta Mathematics Four, 12 on Beta Three, nine on Beta Two and six on Beta One. At each level the children were working on the sections of these books concerned with graphs, which enables Mr A to include occasional class lessons on the work in which everyone can participate. He directs the children's mathematics by assignment cards that tell the children which pages of their books to work on. Other mathematics class books are used from time to time as the occasion warrants.

Other subjects
Activities in the fields of science, music, geography etc. develop through work cards. The four groups are engaged in different subjects at the same time. Mr A organizes the rotation of work in such a way that the groups who are least competent in reading skills get more experience at comprehension and reading.

A theory of classroom organizational strategies

Conceptual background

Reading the research literature (in 1977), I could find no coherent account of the different classroom strategies in primary schools as I observed them in Nottinghamshire. The delightful study by the NFER of 129 teachers in 66 Surrey junior schools (Hilsum and Cane 1971) gave a great deal of information about junior teachers' tasks and the times spent on them, but not about how the children were organized. Bennett's *Teaching Styles and Pupils' Progress* (1976) gave little insight into organizational patterns: the concepts of 'formal' and 'informal' were about teaching style, not classroom organization. Barker Lunn's study, *Streaming in the Primary School* (1970), identified four methods of organization of classes: whole-class teaching, similar ability grouping, mixed ability grouping and the individual approach. This gave me a lead but I saw the curriculum subject rather than children's ability as the organizational basis in the classrooms that I was visiting. The professional literature had a number of accounts of particular ways of organizing classes (for example, Ridgway and Lawton 1968; Brown and Precious 1968), but nothing that I found gave a synoptic overview linking curriculum to organization.

A hypothesis used to analyse the case studies: leading to a fuzzy proposition

I decided to focus on what all the children in a class were doing during a given period of time and in relation to the 'subjects' of the school curriculum. This led to a hypothesis that there were four major organizational strategies operating in these different classrooms. I labelled them: 'classwork in one subject', 'groupwork in one subject', 'groupwork in several subjects' and 'individual work'.[4] As the following analysis of the three different days shows, this categorization covered all the teaching time spent in the classrooms, and so I felt it 'worked'.

1 *Classwork in one subject:* when the attention of the class is on the same work, either individually or collectively. All three teachers used this strategy.

Mrs M

09.03–09.15	Registration and dinner money used for number and language experience involving everyone.
09.30–09.43	Everyone discussing weather and classroom clock and receiving instructions.
10.14–10.30	Tables 4 and 2 reporting to everyone on what they have done.
10.45–11.23	Class discussion: pussy willow, news time; then instructions.
11.50–11.59	Instructions to everyone and class focus on work of table 4.
13.15–13.35	Number questions for everyone, look at class story book, instructions.
14.27–14.40	Class discussion about what has been done this afternoon.
14.53–15.15	Class story time, colour practice, prayers.

Mrs W

09.07–09.32	Registration, dinner money, class discussion about plants, calendar work and instructions.
10.17–10.32	Biscuits and number work, instructions.
13.34–13.50	Class discussion about weather, instructions.
14.50–15.00	Class tidy up room.
15.00–15.25	Showing time, story.

Mr A

09.00–09.10	Registration and individual silent reading.

10.05–10.40	Class discussion of work in progress and then about capital punishment.
13.15–13.44	Registration and individual silent reading.
15.35–15.45	Spelling practice and then story.

2 *Groupwork in one subject:* when only one subject is in progress, but different groups are engaged in different aspects of it, either individually or collectively within groups. Mrs M and Mr A used this strategy.

Mrs M

09.43–10.14	All engaged in mathematics: table 1, sets; table 2, 'hands'; table 3, sequences; table 4, number track; table 5, take aways.
11.20–11.55	All engaged in English: tables 1, 3 and 5, work cards; table 2, story writing; table 4, pictures for phonics.

Mr A

10.55–12.00	All engaged in mathematics of graphs but at four different levels in the Beta Maths books: four groups.

3 *Groupwork in several subjects:* when different groups are engaged in different subjects. Only Mr A used this strategy.

Mr A

13.44–14.30	Group 1, poetry; group 2, encyclopaedias; group 3, topic; group 4, dictionaries; group 5, cooking.
14.50–15.35	Group 1, science; group 2, mapwork; group 3, music; group 4, poetry.

4 *Individual work in several subjects:* when children are engaged in individual studies in different subjects and without any regular groupings. Mrs M and Mrs W used this strategy.

Mrs M

13.35–14.27	Various creative and play activities. Mrs M hears children read.

Mrs W

09.32–10.17	Writing, mathematics, play etc. Mrs W hears children read.
13.50–14.30	Writing, mathematics, play etc. Mrs W hears children read.

In the language that I am now recommending, this successful testing of a hypothesis can lead to the formulation of a fuzzy proposition:

the work of primary classrooms may be analysable into at least four organizational strategies: classwork in one subject, groupwork in one subject, groupwork in several subjects and individual work (with the definitions given above).

It might seem hazardous to base a proposition on such limited evidence, but it was supported by a great deal of my own and colleagues' experience of classrooms. In effect, what these studies did was to record in detail knowledge that was typical and familiar to many teachers and college tutors, but which had not, at that time, been analysed and codified in this particular way. Soon afterwards I was able to test this proposition on a large number of primary schools in Nottinghamshire.

Testing the fuzzy proposition

In the autumn of 1976, for the first time, many newly qualified teachers leaving college were without jobs. At Trent Polytechnic we obtained funding from the Manpower Services Commission for a job creation programme in which 25 of our just-qualified but unemployed students, and subsequently others, joined me to form the Nottinghamshire Primary Schools Research Project team. Overall we interviewed 893 teachers (including heads) in 114 primary schools. The general procedure was that the research officers worked in pairs so that one took the class while the other interviewed the teacher. The research officers were all qualified, if inexperienced, teachers and there was tremendous support for them in their plight from the teachers they interviewed, who gave generously of their time.

One question asked of 498 junior teachers was: 'How much time does a typical pupil spend in a week on each of these four classroom methods?' Because the question was asked in a structured interview the interviewer could spend time explaining the categorization, in these terms:

- *Classwork*: Periods of time when the attention of the class is on the same work, either individually or collectively, e.g. teacher giving instruction on mathematics to everyone, all children doing sums individually from blackboard or workbooks, teacher reading story, all children painting, all children writing stories.
- *Groupwork in one subject*: Periods of time when only one subject is in progress but different groups are engaged in different aspects of it, either individually or collectively within the groups, e.g. one group working individually on sums from 'The 4 Rules of Number', a second group working cooperatively in measuring the classroom, a third group engaged on work cards on shape and a fourth group doing practical work with the teacher on capacity.
- *Groupwork in more than one subject*: Periods of time when different groups are engaged in different subjects, e.g. one group is working on mathematics, a second group is writing stories and a third group is doing some creative work.

- *Self-organized individual work on assignments*: Periods of time when children are engaged in individual studies across the curriculum, which they have chosen to work at from a list of teacher-set assignments.

It was pleasing to find that this categorization worked. Ninety-three per cent of the teachers were able to respond in these terms, as Table 9.1 shows.

Table 9.1 Time spent by a typical pupil in different classroom organizational strategies in 498 junior classrooms in Nottinghamshire in 1976/7 (percentages; rows total 100 per cent)

	$1/4$ to 6 hr per wk	$6^1/4$ to 10 hr per wk	$10^1/4$ plus hr per wk	Not used	No answer
Classwork	26	36	30	1	7
Group work in one subject	48	18	12	15	7
Group work in more than one subject	36	14	10	33	7
Self-organized individual work: assignments	38	9	9	37	7
Other approaches	15	0	0	71	14

The related question asked of infant teachers was posed slightly differently: 'What organizational pattern do you use at present for "activity time"?' Three patterns were explained by the interviewers, as follows, with the recognition that more than one pattern might be used (see Table 9.2).

- *Pattern 1*. This is where the *whole class* starts to do 'mathematics' at the same time (all doing the same, or working in groups, or working individually), and likewise starts to do 'writing' at another time and so on.
- *Pattern 2*. This is where the class is divided into *groups with fixed membership* and one group starts work with 'mathematics', while another starts with 'writing' and another starts with 'art', for example.
- *Pattern 3*. This is where *individual decisions* are made at each activity time for each child (either by the child or by the teacher) as to whether the work is to be 'mathematics', 'writing', 'art' etc.

Again, the classification worked. Although differently expressed, the infant teachers were using the same sort of organizational strategies as the junior teachers.

In simple terms, the outcome of this survey is in accord with the three case studies and can be expressed in the following fuzzy generalization.

Table 9.2 Patterns of classroom organization used by 281 infant teachers in Nottinghamshire in 1976/7 (percentages; column totals 100 per cent)

Pattern 1	Whole class working at same activity – together, in groups, or individually	4
Patterns 1 and 2	See above and below	3
Pattern 2	Class divided into fixed groups which are working at different activities	15
Patterns 2 and 3	See above and below	33
Pattern 3	Individual decisions about activities made by teacher or by child	42
Can't answer		3

It is likely that the organization of most primary school classrooms can be described in terms of some or all of four major organizational strategies: classwork in one subject, groupwork in one subject, groupwork in several subjects and individual work (with the definitions given above).

The survey was in Nottinghamshire in the late 1970s. The empirical findings refer, of course, to particular schools at a particular time. These findings could not legitimately be extrapolated to make a statistical generalization. But a major contention of this book is that they can be expressed as a fuzzy generalization: the modifiers 'it is likely' and 'most' make this possible.

Endpiece

Research is a frustrating activity. Expressed as a story, the above conclusion flows more or less neatly (I believe) from the evidence. At the time it wasn't really like that. It was reported in three books (Bassey 1978a, b, 1989) but only as a small issue. I failed to put together the case studies and the survey data in the way I have here – and perhaps in consequence neither the academic community of researchers nor the professional community of teachers noticed it. I tried to get a research council grant to map the extent to which these four strategies were used in different parts of the country – and was not successful.

I thought the identification of these strategies was important for the reason that I expressed in the report of the Nottinghamshire project.

Few teachers know how other teachers teach. Each teacher develops ways of organising her class more or less on her own and with little opportunity for knowing how other teachers carry out the same tasks. . . . There are no universal 'best methods' in teaching. For a particular teacher with a particular class working in a particular teaching space at a particular time, one method of organisation . . . may be best. For the same teacher with another class, or in another teaching space, or at another time, something different may be best. The decision as to what is the most appropriate method . . . [should] lie with the individual teacher; her excellence at making such decisions depends in part upon the extent to which she knows the options open to her . . . My hope is that the report will help make teachers more aware of the variety of practices in common use and so widen the base from which their classroom decisions are made.

(Bassey 1978a: 9–11)

Today it is my view, regrettably, that much of that freedom of action is disappearing. The pressures of national curriculum, Ofsted inspections, Teacher Training Agency control of teacher qualifications and national literacy and numeracy hours are gradually changing the nature of teachers' work. The teachers are told what to teach, what targets to reach and are beginning to be told how to teach. They are inspected, the children are tested and the results feature in local newspaper reports and public league tables. Teachers are being changed from inspired professionals who educate children so that they can lead worthwhile and creative lives, into instructed technicians who train pupils so that they can become efficient wealth-creating units.

The merit today of case studies like the three reported here, I consider, is as evidence that before the Education Reform Act of 1988 and the subsequent and continuing interference of the state in classrooms, there were dedicated and competent teachers fully committed to the needs of the children in their care who were quite able to work effectively without official monitoring and state harassment.

Notes

1 These three are on different sites but all focus on the same issue of classroom organization. Some would call the overall case study a 'multi-site study'.
2 They were reported in *Practical Classroom Organisation in the Primary School* (1978, Ward Lock) and *Nine Hundred Primary School Teachers* (1978, NFER), but to my regret not brought together in the way constructed here. Here I have used them to support a fuzzy generalization about four organizational strategies found in primary schools. Some of the detail could perhaps have been omitted, but this would have detracted from the richness of the accounts and weakened the evidence that these teachers were highly competent professionals who had carefully thought through their pattern of work in the classroom.
3 The Ward Lock book, and its successor *Teaching Practice in the Primary School* (1989, Ward Lock, now out of print) recommended a four-stage process through which students might reach this level of professional competence.
4 As noted before, it seems impossible to know precisely how, or when, one comes to invent a hypothesis. How far it was influenced by Barker Lunn's study I don't know. Was it in mind before the school studies? What was important was that using it to analyse the case studies worked.

10 | What it is like to be a student on final teaching practice: a picture-drawing case study[1] of fiction firmly based on fact

Abstract

This is an extract from a study of the interface between college, local authority and student in the education and training of primary school teachers, which was carried out and first reported in the academic year 1986/7. The extract is a picture-drawing case study which portrays the intensity of experience of teaching practice for final students and some of the ways in which the uneasy relationship between school and college impinges on that experience. The report is a fictional reconstruction of a student's experience, expressed in a letter to her friend Emma: it is drawn from five in-depth interviews and each point made is supported by detailed analysis of the interview data. The interviews were conducted in Sheffield by a seconded primary school headteacher. Twelve years later, this research still stands up as a clear statement of what is needed in training a young person for a career in primary school. There needs to be a coherent team effort in which the school providing a placement, and the college preparing the student, work closely together and plan, execute and monitor with enormous care the whole experience. This partnership is essential if the student is to develop both self-confidence as a teacher and professional expertise in the classroom. It is very demanding of both school and college to orchestrate this effectively.

Preamble

In 1986/7 Sheila Hall (SRH), an experienced Sheffield primary school headteacher, was seconded by her authority to Nottingham Polytechnic to work with me for a year on 'the problems of teacher education'. We decided to focus on the relationship between college, LEA and school, and how this could develop. From the start we were bemused as to the most effective way of reporting whatever findings arose. We decided early on to use a fictional approach and to ensure that it was firmly based on fact. What follows is extracted from the 174-page report that marked the completion of the research (Hall and Bassey 1987). Since that time there has been enormous upheaval in teacher education, with even the name returning to an earlier label of 'teacher training'. But the issues dealt with in the case study – of the intensity of experience of teaching practice and the uneasy relationships between school and college – remain. One of the partners of this study – the LEA – has been almost removed from the teacher education scene by a succession of central government actions. The significance of this study in the present book is as an illustration of fictional approaches to publishing findings.

Introduction

Three agencies are involved in the overall process of teacher education: the colleges, the education authorities and the schools. The colleges train them, the authorities employ them and the schools use them. But that is too simple, for the schools contribute to initial training, the colleges contribute to selection for employment, the authorities and schools provide induction training and all three contribute to in-service training. In other words, colleges, education authorities and schools interact in the total process of training teachers.

This is the report of an enquiry into the ways in which college, school and authority interact in the training of primary school teachers. Rather than assume that there is a partnership, we refer to the interfaces. In particular, we have examined the interfaces between college, school and authority at the time of the final teaching practice of the college student and at the time of selection, arrival and induction of the new teacher.

What does it feel like to be a student on final teaching practice, and to be a new teacher just starting at school? What support is forthcoming from school, college and authority? How effectively do students and teachers feel they are trained? How do school teachers and college tutors interact in relation to students on teaching practice? What communication is there about the new teacher from college to school? These questions provided the framework of the enquiry.

The enquiry centred on one college, one education authority and a group of primary schools within the authority which provide the college with teaching practice places and have teachers who trained at the college. Data were collected in interviews with 59 people: students, teachers, headteachers, tutors, advisers and administrators. The interviewees were an opportunity sample, but nevertheless chosen as far as possible as being typical of their group. Each interviewee was assured anonymity and had the opportunity to amend, or to withdraw from the record, the write-up of the interview. In the event only a few modifications were made and none of the records was withdrawn. In most cases interviews were conducted at the workplace of the interviewee. All the interviews were carried out by SRH.

How the findings were reported

The initial findings were reported (Hall and Bassey 1987) in a fictionalized form as four letters ('Dear Emma'), as a playlet in two acts ('Meanwhile') and as diary extracts ('The Diary of a Headteacher'). The first act of the playlet was set in a school staffroom, with three teachers and the head discussing students on teaching practice in relation to the problems of the school; the second act was set in a college common room, with three tutors engaged in similar discussion. This was also available as a tape recording. Extensive notes, which analysed the interviews, were included in the report as evidence in support of these fictional accounts and these were also validated by the groups who provided the data on which they are based. There is only space in this truncated account to give the first of the 'Dear Emma' letters.

Reflecting on the findings, we searched for ways in which the interfaces between college, school and university could be changed to improve the training process. Our interim conclusions were expressed in two identical memoranda ('Improving teacher education through the interface between colleges, schools and the LEAs') addressed, in simulation, to the College Board of Studies and the Chief Education Officer's Consultative Group. These memoranda were the subject of further interviews and these are reported, again in fictionalized form, with extensive supporting notes, in a second playlet in two acts ('Yes, But'). Reflecting on these findings, we modified one of the interim conclusions. Finally, we presented in the last section of the report three structural proposals for the improvement of the training process. Again, these parts are omitted from this account: the structural proposals have been overtaken by events.

The fictionalized form of presentation was used for three reasons: it enabled several accounts to be condensed into one, it permitted potentially defamatory statements to be delocalized and, it was hoped, it grasped the reader's attention. It also enabled us, in the four letters to Emma, to change cross-sectional data, from three different generations of student teachers, into a simulated longitudinal account of one person's experience.

The first of the 'Dear Emma' letters is given here, and the subsequent account aims to justify the main ideas in the letter in terms of interview data.

Dear Emma

Well, here I am – final teaching practice has finished. I have just about collapsed and I thought I would write while everything is still clear in my mind. This teaching practice has assumed tremendous importance – the culmination of all I've learned in college and on other teaching practices and perhaps, an indication of what it will be like when I finally get into a school. The beginning of a teaching practice is always nerve-wracking despite previous experiences as schools are so different. There was plenty of time to prepare for this one and in most areas of the curriculum I felt I had a good grounding. Some college courses did more for me than others. I felt that the background was good – it's just that it doesn't always link up with the reality. I was able to plan the work but felt that it was my general organization that let me down. I'd been given models but, as always, adapting them to the school situation was no easy task. I do think that it is beneficial to have had teaching experience in a variety of different situations. Discipline can be a problem. You've heard a bit about children being disruptive but you don't always know how to use that knowledge in a practical way. Fortunately I've usually found that the teachers are helpful, but at the back of my mind is the thought that one day I'll be on my own. I try to assess what I'm doing but I wonder if I'm too critical. Everything has to be perfect! I put comments in my file but I feel that it's all rather negative. Probably the hardest thing is making sure that the work is at the right level for the children. The class teacher helps me with this but, again the thought – 'Next time I'll be on my own!' You begin the teaching practice thinking that you've got it all planned, but what you think you can do doesn't always fit in with the ethos of the school and then panic sets in. It's no use thinking that you can adhere strictly to all that you've been taught. Flexibility is the keynote! I tried to think out what my priority would be, bearing in mind past experiences. I couldn't decide. So many things are important – learning children's names, building up relationships, keeping the children busy with appropriate work, seeing them make progress, maintaining discipline. The list is endless. There have been some disappointments. I haven't always been able to be involved in some areas of the curriculum as much as I would have liked. To balance that there have been surprises. Success in curriculum areas where I felt that I had no confidence. Sometimes I feel that I desperately need someone to talk to. At first it was friends, then as I became more confident I could talk things over with the class teacher. You really need people in the same situation as yourself. They understand. The first day or two I was very nervous about being placed on my own. No other students around. I've decided now that it has been beneficial. I'm not being compared with anyone so it takes the pressure off. You also have to make an effort to mix with the other staff. I've tried to think about the things that have given me confidence – that have been of the most value. A few lectures have given me a good start, but it's been meeting people and being in schools that has made such a difference. I think I've been lucky. My class teacher listened to me and gave support and my tutor came to see me and offered helpful advice. One of my friends wasn't so lucky. She felt a burden in school and her tutor wasn't always available to help. You need constructive advice to help you evaluate in a positive way. Most of all it's being in school, feeling the atmosphere, being with people doing the job. At times I think we all have thought 'Is this what I really want to do?' To have a good teaching practice gives you confidence despite all the pressures to excel at everything. I'm fairly certain that I couldn't keep up this pace. The class teacher is there to keep an eye on things. There's also the thought that you don't want to be remembered for leaving chaos when you hand back the class to their own teacher. If everything goes well I will soon be teaching my own class. No opportunities then to give them back to somebody else. My responsibility – a daunting thought but a challenge! I'll let you know what it's like.

Love
S

Internal evidence of trustworthiness

Five fourth-year BEd students had been interviewed in school by SRH towards the end of their final teaching practice and the findings were expressed in the *Dear Emma: teaching practice letter*. This section shows how ten key sentences in the letter are actually analytical statements drawn from rigorous analysis of the interview reports. Headings are taken from the 'Dear Emma' letter. Other quotations are taken from the interviews. These notes were published in the final report in 1987 as evidence of the trustworthiness of the 'Dear Emma' letter: they contain five times as many words.

'There was plenty of time to prepare and in most areas of the curriculum I felt I had a good grounding.'

The timing of this teaching practice, in the early part of the autumn term, and the fact that the students made their initial visits before the summer holiday, allowed plenty of time for preparation. In some schools the class arrangements had not been finalized, so the students on their first visit were able to discover only general information at that time rather than specific arrangements for the class that they would be teaching.

The students felt that they had been prepared for teaching practice by a combination of college courses and experience in schools. One commented that making a choice of age group at the end of the second year had given them the advantage of concentration on that age group for a full year before starting on their final teaching practice.

Some college courses had made them feel confident because not only had they developed their own knowledge of a curriculum area but they had also been taught how to use that knowledge in working with children. Other college courses had been disappointing because they felt that the work was at the student level with no indication of how to apply their knowledge to their work in school.

It depends on which group you are in.

One student made that comment and remarks made by the other students showed that in some areas of the curriculum students had had very different experiences. They also had different reactions if they had shared the same experience.

College stresses creative writing then you go out into school and find that you need phonics.

I had no idea how to set up a creative writing lesson.

I enjoy creative writing and I have introduced poetry.

I feel happy about teaching reading.

I don't feel prepared for teaching those who need help with reading.

I gained my knowledge of early reading from teaching practice.

I felt prepared for teaching music this time.

I was not prepared for teaching music – it was more geared to students.

In Industry Week we worked at our own level in music. That helped.

Previously music was aimed at people with no musical ability. There was no progression. I felt less able to teach music last time.

It should be my strong point but I don't know where to start with children who've had no musical experience.

Despite the fact that the students thought that some courses were particularly good, they sometimes had problems when they were in school.

Although I felt that the PE course was good I dreaded games. The children were better than me.

The PE lectures were good but then I get in the hall and I'm put off by work on the apparatus.

There was general agreement that the students needed to be in school working with children and seeing class teachers working so that they could use all the information that they had been given by their college lectures.

Any knowledge about practical work has come from teaching practice.

I'm worried about children with special needs. I don't know the progression. When I did an assignment in school the teachers had to help me.

We weren't actually told how to teach children with special needs. I found out a lot about children with special needs on teaching practice.

On this final teaching practice I have picked up a lot.

'I felt that it was my general organization that let me down'

This was an area in which the students did not feel well prepared. Their worries covered a wide range, from organizing the children in the class to organizing their own time to make displays and to knowing about administration matters such as class registers. A problem in preparing the students to cope with classroom organization is the fact that schools differ widely in the way in which they are organized. The methods of team teaching, working an integrated day or working with groups within the class can be interpreted in different ways so there is not one correct model, but even allowing for this the students felt that they could have been better prepared by college.

We were not helped at all. We were given a model but not helped to work out exactly how to put it into practice.

Teaching practice has helped to sort out different kinds of organization.

Team teaching threw me. In terms of college work there was no preparation.

The biggest problem was with team teaching. You don't know how much sound and movement is allowed. It can be difficult with two to three other people listening, although in some ways it can be a help.

In a team teaching situation my first thought was 'I can't do it'. All those children, all the records, learning names. Nothing to hang on to as your own lesson.

The basis was to follow the college way but we weren't always told how to put it into action.

We've had no instruction or college lectures on classroom organization.

More general matters of organization are important to the smooth running of the school day. Some schools are more prepared than others to involve the students in daily administrative duties.

> We had no preparation for anything on the admin side such as registers, but I've done registers on teaching practice.

In the busy working day in school everyone's time must be used effectively, and forward planning had to include making time for using the available resource equipment and preparing displays.

> We were very lacking in preparation for organization such as putting up displays, doing dinner books, techniques of writing on the blackboard and using the banda.

'Everything has to be perfect'

> Every lesson has to be perfect – that's the expectation of college tutors.

There is a lot of pressure to be seen to be doing well. In the comparatively short period of teaching practice there does not appear to be any room for things going wrong and having to rethink the approach. By the time a student has started again precious days have been lost. The students were conscious that their planning was of the utmost importance and in this respect they felt that they had been well prepared by the college.

> I was quite confident.

> My main aim is to plan. Even if everything doesn't go according to plan there is a springboard.

> The best thing has been clear instruction on how to set out a file. You know what you have to do to please the tutor.

> I felt very well prepared by college for planning my work.

The students were less happy about planning appropriate work for the children. They began the teaching practice not knowing any of the children and had to rely on help from the class teacher in planning appropriate work.

> It's the hardest thing. I don't feel very confident.

> There was not a lot done in college, but I have no problems in school. The class teacher is there to check that the work is the right level.

The students relied on feedback from college tutors and class teachers in order to evaluate the work that they were doing. They felt the pressure to do well and to be seen to be achieving results, and in some cases they were over-anxious or too self-critical.

A lot of work had been done on it and it has worked – perhaps too well. I find I am too critical about myself.

Self-evaluation is more a matter of self-awareness and maturity than being taught.

The tutor says the evaluation in my file is good. I try to be very self-critical and ask questions. It's not a lot of help if the tutor says that the evaluation is good and doesn't discuss it. When you've asked the question you need an answer.

It's a problem this year. The tutor is helpful but sceptical and vague about assessment.

The headteacher says I'm far too critical. It's not always a good idea to criticize yourself too much.

At college we're made to look at what is not so good. We don't look at the positive good things.

'What you think you can do doesn't always fit in with the ethos of the school'

College gives you an ideal scheme of work. You have to have a reason for doing your lesson. There's not a lot of time for flexibility or impulse.

The students acknowledged the help that had been given to them in preparing them for the teaching practice, but in some instances they had felt unprepared for the flexibility that can occur in school. Some of them did not feel able to cope if the work was not going according to plan. If the children didn't react as they expected the students were hesitant about changing their plans.

Initially I thought I would be able to do things then I found for different reasons that I was not able to.

There were some disappointments. The students were eager to include their own special interests and did not always have the opportunity to do so.

I could only do music for twenty minutes a week.

I only used the computer once.

I would have liked to do CDT but one of the teachers had been on a course so I didn't get the chance.

The students are prepared in college to go out into a variety of schools in different areas of the city. Each school has its own identity, its own pattern of organization and ideas about the appropriate teaching methods for that school. Some of the students had heard from fellow students that it was difficult to work informally in a formal school, but had not necessarily experienced that situation themselves. All the students realized that they could not be prepared for every situation that they were likely to encounter, but they looked for support where college and school expectations differed. Not all the students felt that they had received such support.

Before the first teaching practice I was told to try to fit into the school's organization.

In the second year it was all formal. The children sat in rows. The tutor said I was to fit into that organization.

The children were used to working formally. I was asked by college to work with groups of children. There was no support from the tutor.

Some of the difficulties were outside the control of the student even though plans had been made in good time.

College expects you to organize trips but it's not easy in school. Sometimes they don't want you to take the children out. Sometimes you're put off by the place you want to visit. It's the time factor. Even if you plan early some places are already fully booked.

'So many things are important'

When interviewed, the students had almost completed their final teaching practice. They were asked what their priorities had been at the start of the practice.

To learn the children's names. Build up relationships.

My aim is to plan even if it doesn't always work.

At the end of the day to see that everyone has progressed in some way.

The student who made that comment had been disappointed because she felt that despite her best efforts the children didn't seem to take a pride in their work, and their art work particularly was slapdash.

For the first two or three weeks keep the children very busy. Maintain discipline.

There were some worries about standards of the children's behaviour in school, and some of the students felt unprepared for dealing with this.

We had no help with discipline at college.

We had some lectures but they made no impact.

We had some information in college about behaviour problems but we were not able to relate it practically.

I don't know how to deal with disruptive children.

Teachers on teaching practice have given ideas for keeping discipline.

On one teaching practice I had a rowdy class. I am very quiet. The teacher shouted at the children and they shouted back. It was generally accepted that it was a noisy class. There's no preparation for this sort of thing. No real help from the tutor.

My priority is that the children see me as a teacher.

One student explained that on the final teaching practice she had had the confidence, even on preliminary visits, to correct children straight away if necessary. The class teacher had supported her in this.

'Sometimes I feel that I desperately need someone to talk to'

One student said that on this final teaching practice she was more self-contained and hadn't felt the need to talk to anyone, but on previous practices she had not been quite so confident. Most of the students said that in the early stages of the practice the greatest support came from talking to other students who were in the same situation as themselves. Some of them were hesitant at first to talk to the teachers.

Now I talk to the teachers. At the beginning of the practice I talked to friends. I was too embarrassed to talk to teachers. You want to look as if you're coping.

On one practice at first I thought the teacher was watching my every move. I was afraid to use my initiative and correct the children.

I know more teachers in the team-teaching situation.

I've never talked about problems to the teacher and headteacher but they've given me positive help.

The students said that many of the tutors were supportive on all occasions, but there were times when some of them would have liked more help from some tutors. The difficulties arose when the supervising tutors were not usually involved in teaching that particular age group, and the students hesitated to ask for advice.

I had a difficult time on one teaching practice but I was able to talk to the tutor.

I've had personal problems and I was able to talk to the tutor.

I've always had tutors who said that everything was fine.

The tutor usually supervises a different age group. I don't feel as though I can ask for help.

I did have an occasion where I felt that the tutor was not supportive.

My tutor doesn't come in very much so there isn't chance to talk.

In some cases students turned to someone outside the school situation when they needed to talk. Friends, relations, landladies provided a sympathetic ear.

'The first day or two I was very nervous about being placed on my own'

All the students interviewed had been the only student in their school on this teaching practice and they were able to compare it with other practices when they had been placed with other students. They all said that after the first few days of settling in the advantages of being on their own far outweighed the disadvantages.

I feel quite confident. Very occasionally I feel on my own. With others you can swap ideas.

It's a lot better on my own even though on the first day I felt nervous and fed-up.

If two are together you feel you are being compared.

Students sit together in the staffroom and talk together.

It's a bonus. On one practice when everything was going badly I felt it was too competitive. Displays were compared.

You get more attention from the staff. You feel less like a student.

I've loved it. It takes the pressure off. There are no comparisons although a bit of competition is not too bad.

You have to make an effort to mix.

It's been a benefit. I almost feel like a member of staff.

'I've tried to think about things that have given me confidence'

The students talked about their preparation in college and how it had helped them when they had gone into schools for teaching practice. They said that in many areas of the curriculum they had been given a good background at their own level but they were most confident when they had been told how to apply that knowledge to teaching children.

It was a good course. I felt well prepared. Had ideas to use in school.

I feel very confident to try out different ways of teaching and to teach through understanding.

Very practical. We were told how to teach.

We were told how to organize the lessons and how to use apparatus. We were shown the progression.

In contrast, their comments showed that some lectures had not been seen as helpful.

You don't always see the relevance of lectures.

It was appalling. Very little on school work.

It was vague and far from reality.

The theory is far from what happens in schools.

Sometimes, because they themselves were particularly good at a subject, they had difficulty in knowing where to start with the children who had had no previous experience.

It should be my strong point, but where do you start with ten-year-olds who have had hardly any musical experience?

Sometimes the students felt that the children were better than they were, especially in P.E. and they were pleasantly surprised when the lessons were a success.

I thought PE was my worst subject. I dreaded it then I found that it was a pleasant surprise.

The students were apprehensive at the beginning of all the teaching practices, particularly if there had been difficulties on a previous occasion.

My confidence was low because of my last teaching practice. Now things are going well I feel much better.

When the students had had an opportunity to work in situations outside their own classroom they felt that they were a part of the school. Some helped with plays or with the orchestra. Some were able to use special equipment such as video cameras. They felt as though they were trusted and treated as responsible people.

The attitude of everyone around was of great importance to them. They needed to feel welcome.

The deputy head helped me with a project then everyone joined in with ideas.

The staff were tremendous.

When I helped with the music for the concert the teacher said it was marvellous to have someone helping.

All the students agreed that the time spent in school was of great value and they could learn a lot if everyone in school supported them.

> If I had to choose one thing that had given me the most confidence I would say that it was school experience.

> This teaching practice has given me confidence. Before I didn't know if I wanted to be a teacher.

> This teaching practice has been of the most value. In fact all teaching practices have been really good.

> Being in school. Teachers I've worked with.

> Team-teaching has been quite hard but good experience. With this organization I know a lot more children and staff. More about the school as a whole. I feel a part of the school.

> Most of all it's being in school, feeling the atmosphere, being with people doing the job.

'One of my friends wasn't so lucky'

The students perceived teaching practice to be a major influence in their training, and where they were well supported by college and school they had found the experience to be of great value. When reflecting on all their teaching practices, the students could quote some examples of occasions when they had felt that not enough effort had been made by either college or school. They had felt very much on their own.

> This time the tutor was supportive, but on one teaching practice the tutor was used to secondary schools and seemed to be uncomfortable with the children.

> There's no set structure. The tutors are all looking for different things. It varies according to who you have.

> My tutor doesn't have the knowledge to help me with PE.

> Over the four years the tutors haven't helped me to improve.

> I've had no real help with discipline. The tutor saw me teach twice.

> I've had occasions where the tutor wasn't used to primary schools and wasn't supportive.

> I was asked by college to do group work in a formal school. It didn't work in that school. The tutor was not supportive and didn't see me teach even though the school phoned.

> One student had no support from college. No written reports.

An extreme case quoted by one student was of a situation where there was conflict between the teaching staff in school. The student was surrounded by antagonism and negative attitudes. Although none of this was directed towards the student and the college tried to give support, the atmosphere in school did not allow the student to feel comfortable.

Most of the school experiences had been positive and helpful but there had been instances when students thought that they were not welcome.

At one school I felt like a burden.

After a lot of time preparing a file the classroom teacher said it should be started again.

The headteacher had not had students in school before.

We didn't go to any staff meetings.

We had twenty minutes in the staffroom at lunchtime then we had to go out.

'Is this really what I want to do?'

The pressure to do well, the pace at which the students were working and the unexpected difficulties that they sometimes encountered contributed to a feeling of being overwhelmed at times during their training. Even some incidents which on reflection seemed unimportant caused anxiety when they occurred at a time when students wanted to be seen to be achieving success.

I felt so much pressure to do a PE lesson really well.

I didn't feel confident. Was I too strict, too controlled?

What do you do to get the children to learn their lines for assembly?

On one teaching practice there was a child who was dreaded by all. I didn't know how to deal with it.

I was ready to give up. No support from anywhere.

I nearly gave up at the end of the third year. I felt the pressure. My family thought that college expected too much.

This final practice has given me confidence. I didn't know before whether I wanted to be a teacher. I'll be sad to leave.

External evidence of trustworthiness

The *Dear Emma: teaching practice* letter was discussed with the five students after the practice when they were back in college. They agreed that the letter 'rang true' in representing the views of students on final teaching practice. In particular, one said, 'This is fine. It brings it all back with startling clarity.' Similar support was obtained from a national conference of teachers and college tutors, organized by HMI to consider the findings of this research, and from smaller events.

In the final report on the project, we wrote:

> Our experiences, as a tutor with 25 years in teacher training (MB), and as a teacher and headteacher with 22 years of teaching in primary schools (SRH), and the supportive comments made at conferences where these results have been presented, lead us to believe that the findings, drawn from one area and a small number of students, are typical of the situation today [1987] throughout the country. Moreover we have found nothing in the two recent surveys by HMI of teacher training to suggest otherwise (*The New Teacher in School*, 1982 and *Quality in Schools: Initial Teacher Training*, 1987).
>
> (Hall and Bassey 1987: 171)

Endpiece

Twelve years later, this research still stands up as a clear statement of what is needed in training a young person for a career in primary school. There needs to be a coherent team effort in which the school providing a placement, and the college preparing the student, work closely together and plan, execute and monitor with enormous care the whole experience. This partnership is essential if the student is to develop both self-confidence as a teacher and professional expertise in the classroom. It is very demanding of both school and college to orchestrate this effectively.

Note

1 To be precise, but too long-winded for a title, this is a story-telling case report which focuses on a picture-drawing case study.

References

Adelman, C., Kemmis, S. and Jenkins, D. (1980) Rethinking case study: notes from the second Cambridge conference. In H. Simon (ed.) *Towards a Science of the Singular*. Norwich: Centre for Applied Research in Education, University of East Anglia, pp. 45–61.

Atkinson, P. and Delamont, S. (1985) Bread and dreams or bread and circuses? A critique of 'case study' research in education. In M. Shipman (ed.) *Educational Research. Principles, Policies and Practices*. London: Falmer, pp. 26–45.

Barker Lunn, J. C. (1970) *Streaming in the Primary School*. Slough: NFER.

Bassey, M. (1978a) *Nine Hundred Primary School Teachers*. Slough: NFER.

Bassey, M. (1978b) *Practical Classroom Organisation in the Primary School*. London: Ward Lock.

Bassey, M. (1980) Crocodiles eat children, *Bulletin of Classroom Action Research Network*.

Bassey, M. (1981) Pedagogic research: on the relative merits of search for generalisation and study of single events, *Oxford Review of Education*, 7(1), 73–94.

Bassey, M. (1983) Pedagogic research into singularities: case-studies, probes and curriculum innovations, *Oxford Review of Education*, 9(2), 109–21.

Bassey, M. (1989) *Teaching Practice in the Primary School*. London: Ward Lock.

Bassey, M. (1992) Creating education through research (Presidential address to BERA), *British Educational Research Journal*, 18(1), 3–16.

Bassey, M. (1995) *Creating Education through Research: a Global Perspective of Educational Research for the 21st Century*. Edinburgh/Newark: British Educational Research Association/Kirklington Moor Press.

Bassey, M. (1998) Enhancing teaching through research, *Professional Development Today*, 1(2), 39–46.

Bassey, M. and Constable, H. (1997) Higher education research in education 1992–1996: fields of enquiry reported in the HEFCs' RAE, *Research Intelligence*, 61, 6–8.

Bennett, N. (1976) *Teaching Styles and Pupil Progress*. Wells: Open Books.

Blatchford, P. and Sumpner, C. (1998) What do we know about breaktime? Results from a national survey of breaktime and lunchtime in primary and secondary schools, *British Educational Research Journal* 24(1), 79–94.

Brown, M. and Precious, N. (1968) *The Integrated Day in the Primary School*. London: Ward Lock.

Brown, S. and McIntyre, D. (1993) *Making Sense of Teaching*. Buckingham: Open University Press.

Cohen, L. and Manion, L. (1989) *Research Methods in Education*, 3rd edn. London: Routledge.

Crossley, M. and Vulliamy, G. (1984) Case-study research methods of comparative education. *Comparative Education*, 20(2), 193–207.

Crossley, M. and Vulliamy, G. (eds) (1997) *Qualitative Research in Developing Countries*. New York: Garland.

DES/HMI (1982) *The New Teacher in School*. London: HMSO.
DES/HMI (1987) *Quality in Schools. Initial Teacher Training*. London: HMSO.
Eliot, T. S. (1944) *Four Quartets*. London: Faber and Faber.
Eraut, M. (1989) Initial teacher training and the NCVQ model. In J. W. Burke (ed.) *Competency Based Education and Training*. Lewes: Falmer.
Fourali, C. (1997) Using fuzzy logic in educational measurement, *Evaluation and Research in Education*, 11(3), 129–48.
Furlong, J. (1990) School based training: the students' views. In M. Booth, J. Furlong and M. Wilkin (eds) *Partnership in Initial Teacher Training*. London: Croom Helm.
Glaser, B. G. and Strauss, A. L. (1967) *The Discovery of Grounded Theory: Strategies for Qualitative Research*. New York: Aldine.
Goldstein, H. (1986) Integration of theory and practice: a humanistic approach, *Social Work*, September/October, 352–6.
Gowin, D.R. (1972) Is educational research distinctive? In L.G.Thomas (ed.) *Philosophical Redirection of Educational Research*, 71st Yearbook of the National Society for the Study of Education. Illinois: University of Chicago Press.
Hall, S. and Bassey, M. (1987) *Teacher Education: the Interface between College, LEA and School*. Nottingham: Trent Polytechnic.
Halpern, E. S. (1983) Auditing naturalistic inquiries: the development and application of a model. Unpublished doctoral dissertation. Indiana University (cited by Lincoln and Guba, 1985).
Hamilton, D., Jenkins, D., King, C., McDonald, B. and Parlett, M. (eds) (1977) *Beyond the Numbers Game: a Reader in Educational Evaluation*. Basingstoke: Macmillan.
Hargreaves, D. H. (1996) *Teaching as a Research-based Profession: Possibilities and Prospects*, Teacher Training Agency Annual Lecture 1996. London: Teacher Training Agency.
Hargreaves, D. H. (1997) Response to Maurice Kogan. In S. Hegarty (ed.) *The Role of Research in Mature Education Systems*. Slough: NFER, pp. 228–32.
Hargreaves, D. H. (1998) Improving research to enhance teaching, *Professional Development Today*, 1(2), 47–55.
Hegarty, S. (ed.) (1997) *The Role of Research in Mature Education Systems*. Slough: National Foundation for Educational Research.
Hilsum, S. and Cane, B. S. (1971) *The Teacher's Day*. Slough: NFER.
HMI (1979) *Developments in the BEd Degree Course: a Study Based on Fifteen Institutions*. London: HMSO.
Holligan, C. (1997) Theory in initial teacher education: students' perspectives on its utility – a case study, *British Educational Research Journal*, 23(4), 533–51.
James Committee (1971) *Teacher Education and Supply*. London: Department of Education and Science.
Jeffreys, M. V. C. (1950) *Glaucon: an Enquiry into the Aims of Education*. London: Pitman.
Keeves, J. P. (ed.) (1985) *Educational Research, Methodology, and Measurement: an International Handbook*, 1st edn. Oxford: Pergamon.
Keeves, J. P. (ed.) (1994) *Educational Research, Methodology, and Measurement: an International Handbook*, 2nd edn. Oxford: Pergamon.
Kemmis, S. (1980) The imagination of the case and the invention of the study. In H. Simons (ed.) *Towards a Science of the Singular*. Norwich: Centre for Applied Research in Education, University of East Anglia, pp. 96–142.
Kosko, B (1994) *Fuzzy Thinking*. London: Harper/Collins.

Labour Party (1991) *Investing in Quality: Labour's Plans to Reform Teacher Education and Training.* London: Labour Party.

Lawlor, S. (1990) *Teachers Mistaught: Training Theories or Education in Subjects?* London: Centre for Policy Studies.

Lincoln, Y. S. and Guba, E. G. (1985) *Naturalistic Inquiry.* Newbury Park, CA: Sage.

Macdonald, B. and Walker, R. (1977) Case-study and the social philosophy of educational research. In D. Hamilton *et al.* (eds) *Beyond the Numbers Game: a Reader in Educational Evaluation.* Basingstoke: Macmillan, pp. 181–9.

Morgan, H. (1997) *Motivation of Sixth-form Students.* London: Teacher Training Agency.

Ofsted/HMI (1993) *The New Teacher in School: a Survey in England and Wales.* London: HMSO.

O'Hear, A. (1988) *Who Teaches the Teachers?* London: Social Affairs Unit.

Parlett, M. and Hamilton, D. (1977) Evaluation as illumination: a new approach to the study of innovatory programmes. In D. Hamilton *et al.* (eds) *Beyond the Numbers Game: a Reader in Educational Evaluation.* Basingstoke: Macmillan, pp. 6–22.

Peters, R. S. (1966) *Ethics and Education.* London: George Allen and Unwin.

Popper, K. (1963) *Conjectures and Refutations.* Oxford: Oxford University Press.

Ridgway, L. and Lawton, I. (1968) *Family Grouping in the Primary School.* London: Ward Lock.

Scottish Education Department (1978) *Learning to Teach: the Sneddon Report.* London: HMSO.

Shipman, M. (ed.) (1985) *Educational Research: Principles, Policies and Practices.* London: Falmer.

Simons, H. (ed.) (1980) *Towards a Science of the Singular.* Norwich: Centre for Applied Research in Education, University of East Anglia.

Simons, H. (1996) The paradox of case study, *Cambridge Journal of Education,* 26(2), 225–40.

Stake, R. E. (1995) *The Art of Case Study Research.* London: Sage.

Stenhouse, L. (1978) Case study and case records: towards a contemporary history of education, *British Educational Research Journal,* 4(2), 21–39.

Stenhouse, L. (1980) The study of samples and the study of cases, *British Educational Research Journal,* 6(1), 1–6.

Stenhouse, L. (1988) Case study methods. In J. P. Keeves (ed.) *Educational Research, Methodology, and Measurement: an International Handbook,* 1st edn. Oxford: Pergamon, pp. 49–53.

Sturman, A. (1994) Case study methods. In J. P. Keeves (ed.) *Educational Research, Methodology, and Measurement: an International Handbook,* 2nd edn. Oxford: Pergamon, pp. 61–6.

Tripp, D. (1985) Case study generalisation: an agenda for action, *British Educational Research Journal,* 11(1), 33–43.

Troyna, B. (1995) Beyond reasonable doubt? Researching 'race' in educational settings, *Oxford Review of Education,* 21(4), 395–408.

Walker, R. (1983) Three good reasons for not doing case studies in curriculum research, *Journal of Curriculum Studies,* 15(2), 155–65.

Yin, R. K. (1993) *Applications of Case Study Research.* London: Sage.

Yin, R. K. (1994) *Case Study Research: Design and Methods,* 2nd edn. London: Sage.

Zeller, N. (1995) Narrative strategies for case study reports, *Qualitative Studies in Education,* 8(1), 75–88.

Index

abstract, 89
action research – a definition, 41
Adelman, C., 22, 23, 30, 31
analytical statements, 70
annotations, 70
archive, 79–80
Atkinson, P., 34–5
audit certificate, 90
audit trail, 61

Blatchford, P., 45
Brown, S., 49–50

case record, 69, 77, 80
case report, 80, 84–90
case study, types of
  evaluative, 63
  picture-drawing, 62–3
  story-telling, 62
  theory-seeking, 62
  theory-testing, 62
claim to knowledge, 89
Cohen, L., 23–4
craft knowledge of politics, 50–51
craft knowledge of teaching, 50–51
Crossley, M., 63

data analysis, 83–4
data collection methods, 81–3
data items, 70
descriptive reporting, 87
discipline research in educational
  settings – a definition, 39

dissertations, problems of, 5–7

education – a framework definition,
  37–8
educational case study – a conceptual
  reconstruction, 58
educational research – a definition,
  38–9
educational research, teaching and
  policy – a model, 50
Eliot, T.S., 36
empirical educational research
  (overview), 4
empirical research – a definition, 40
evaluation: formative and summative,
  110–12
evaluative case studies, 63
evaluative research – a definition,
  41

fictional reporting, 88
fields of educational research in the
  RAE of 1996, 7–9
Fourali, C., 46
fuzzy generalization, 12, 51–4
fuzzy proposition, 13

generalization, types of:
  fuzzy, 12, 51–4
  scientific, 12, 44
  statistical, 12, 31, 45
genuflection (frippery of style), 6
Gowin, D.R., 45

Hall, S.R., 158–73
Hargreaves, D.H., 11, 48–9, 55–6
Holligan, C., 14–19

illuminative evaluation, 28–9, 34
Internet, 55
interpretive research paradigm, 43

Kemmis, S., 24–5, 59
kingmaking (frippery of style), 6
Kosko, B., 46

Lincoln, Y.S., 75, 76, 77

MacDonald, B., 24
Morgan, H., 52–3

narrative reporting, 86

Parlett, M., 28–9
partisanship, 90
picture-drawing case study, 62–3
polemics, 90
positivist research paradigm, 42

research – a definition, 38
Research Assessment Exercise (RAE),
    7–11
research ethics, 73
research hypothesis, 66

research issue, 67
research problem, 66–7
research questions, 67
respect for democracy, 74
respect for persons, 74, 77–9
respect for truth, 74

sandbagging (frippery of style), 6
Simons, H., 22, 36, 110
singularity – a definition, 47
stages of case study research
    (summary), 66
Stake, R.E., 27, 29–30, 32–3
Stenhouse, L., 25–6, 27–8, 31–2, 77,
    79
story-telling case study, 62
Sturman, A., 26

Teacher Training Agency, 53–4
theoretical research – a definition,
    40–41
theory-seeking case study, 62
theory-testing case study, 62
Tripp, D., 33–4
Troyna, B., 90
trustworthiness, 74–7

Walker, R., 35

Yin, R.K., 26–7, 29, 31, 34